Tragedy
and
the Theory
of Drama

Books by Elder Olson

Verse
====

Thing of Sorrow
Cock of Heaven
The Scarecrow Christ
Plays and Poems: 1948–1958

Criticism
=====

Critics and Criticism: Ancient and
Modern
(*Co-author with R. S. Crane, R. P. Mc-
Keon, and others*)
The Poetry of Dylan Thomas

Elder Olson

Tragedy
and
the Theory
of Drama

Wayne State University Press
Detroit 1961

For Joseph Randall Shapiro
and his wife Jorie

Contents

Introduction

THIS BOOK grew out of lectures—primarily a series of lectures on tragedy delivered at Wayne State University in the spring of 1958, but also others given at the University of Texas, Drake University, and Indiana University. It is a book of which I shall always be fond, for it must remind me of the many kindnesses I was shown in all of these universities. I take particular pleasure, consequently, in dedicating it to two persons who are the very essence of kindness.

I wrote it to fill what seemed to me a certain need. There are many excellent manuals on stage-craft, playwriting, and other aspects of dramatic art, and there is a very great deal of sound dramatic criticism; but there has been little inquiry into dramatic principles themselves. The *word* "principles" appears very frequently in the titles of books on the drama, but almost invariably it has the meaning of *rules, hints, rudiments* —in short, of nearly everything but principles in the sense of those ultimates which underlie both the theory and the practice of the art. We talk constantly about plays, about dramatic action, about the technical resources of dramatic art; but perhaps we should be hard put to it to say exactly what we mean by these. I wanted to discover what we do mean, perhaps ought to mean; and I have attempted to see tragedy—indeed, as much as possible of the whole of drama—from a point of view which is seldom taken: the point of view of the working dramatist. The problems of the dramatist, the technical means for their solution, the principles governing the different methods of solution comprise the subject of this book.

By an inquiry into principles I hoped chiefly to liberalize my own views: to free myself from prejudices and assumptions that had no better foundation than my own inertia and no better warrant than habit, and so to liberalize my own tastes as well. I have the feeling now that I did manage to liberalize my views and tastes a little, and I am encouraged thus to hope that this study may have a similar effect on others.

"An inquiry into principles" is likely to sound difficult, dull, and dogmatic. Since I seem to be in a sanguine mood, I shall hope also that this book is none of these. I have done my best to make difficult inquiry as easy as possible; and I have tried, at least, to avoid being dull. I have tried, too, to avoid being dogmatic. If I have failed in this last, I ask the reader to bear in mind my good intentions, and to consider all of my dogmas as no more than themes for his consideration.

Elder Olson

January, 1961

2

I
Drama and
Dramatic Action

ONCE UPON A TIME (it seems as long ago as that!) when
I was an undergraduate, a young teacher attempted to
introduce us young barbarians to the glories of Aeschylus' *Agamemnon*—indeed, of the whole *Oresteia*.
He was an excellent teacher in every way, and he did
his very best. He told us about the Greeks and the development of Greek drama, and initiated us into some
of the more obvious mysteries of Aristotle's *Poetics*.
We listened with pleasure and took notes with industry; and we were convinced of the truth of everything he said (quite properly, for it happened to be
true)—except for one small point. This small point,
however, he regarded as the chief or rather the only
point of the whole course: in his view, the course was
meaningless unless we had come to see the greatness
of the *Agamemnon* as drama, and of Aeschylus as
dramatist.

That greatness we were unwilling to concede. Most
of us felt that *Mourning Becomes Electra* was far better
than the *Oresteia;* and of course the latest Garbo movie
was better still. As for Aeschylus and, for that matter,

3

Sophocles and Euripides, we thought their efforts interesting but primitive. We could look at them with indulgence (the indulgence with which an aircraft engineer might look upon the efforts of a caveman to produce a wheel); but *greatness?* Nonsense; the Greeks had simply got in on the ground floor again, as they seemed to have done in almost everything; and perhaps they had held their own through critical inertia or an academic conspiracy of some sort.

At one point in the rather animated discussion the instructor tried to make his case by reading us A. E. Housman's parody of Greek tragedy. He had the interesting theory that parody can sometimes bring insights where straightforward discussion fails—much, he said, as caricature can often disclose something that portraiture cannot. Housman's parody is a wonderful one, and we particularly enjoyed the part where Eriphyla—very much like Agamemnon—is being murdered within doors, off-stage. She does not care for the process any more than Agamemnon did, and she makes this perfectly clear. The Chorus stands outside and makes some comments of its own.

> ERI.: O, I am smitten with a hatchet's jaw;
> And that in deed and not in word alone.
> CHO.: I thought I heard a sound within the house
> Unlike the voice of one that jumps for joy.
> ERI.: He splits my skull, not in a friendly way,
> Once more; he purposes to kill me dead.
> CHO.: I would not be reputed rash, but yet
> I doubt if all be gay within the house.
> ERI.: O! O! Another stroke! that makes the third.
> He stabs me to the heart against my wish.

4

CHO.: If that be so, thy state of health is poor,
    But thine arithmetic is quite correct.

The device of parody backfired. We thought that
this caught the absurdity of Greek drama precisely. It
established our case beyond doubt.

Yes; Greek tragedy was absurd. Just look at the
Agamemnon, for instance: the watchman appears, sees
the signal fires which mean that Troy has fallen, utters
a dark hint or two, and disappears forever from the
play. The Chorus enters and offers, by way of entertainment, a history of the Trojan war, with a long
special appendix on the sacrifice of Iphigenia. Clytemnestra enters and interprets the signal fires quite
correctly; and the Chorus refuses to believe her, apparently on no better ground than that she is merely
a woman. A herald comes in, tells them the same
thing, and they believe him (he, you see, is a *man*).
The play is half over before Agamemnon appears. He
becomes immediately involved in an argument with
Clytemnestra over the interesting question of whether
he will or will not walk on the red carpets which she
has spread for him. He proves conclusively that he
ought not to, and then does walk on them after all, of
course, for he is a married man. (As a famous logician
once said to me, "I win all the arguments in our house,
but my wife wins all the fights.") Cassandra finally
speaks, and we have one of the greatest failures of com-
munication in history. Presently, from off-stage, Agamemnon gives us a blow-by-blow account of his own
murder. And that is pretty much that.

A great tragedy? A great play? No, no, certainly not

5

great, and almost as certainly, not a tragedy; perhaps not even a play. For how could it be tragedy? The only incident in it that might have had tragic force is the murder of Agamemnon; but too little is shown of him too late in the play for any great tragic effect, and even that little does not make him sympathetic. How could this sort of thing be called a play, except in the broadest sense? There was hardly any action, and the greater part of that, we thought, was not *dramatic* action. Where were the climaxes piled on climaxes, the unexpected turns, the startling discoveries, the surprising denouement?

You will have decided by now that we were either very wrong-headed or very recalcitrant students. I will say one thing in our defense: knowing no Greek, we were laboring with a somewhat discouraging translation. It is very difficult to feel the sublimity of the *Agamemnon,* or to be much cheered by the information that it is better in the Greek, when you are reading lines like these:

> O Helen! Helen! Phrenzied Helen!
> Many hearts of thee are telling!

Or these:

> Self-will, fell Até's daughter, still
>   Fore-counselling ruin,
> Shall spur him on resistless borne
>   To his undoing.

But the real trouble lay much deeper than that. It lay in the fact that we were quite certain what tragedy was; that we were quite certain what a play was; and that, certain and assured as we were, we were wrong.

What is a play? The answer is a simple one for the young or for the simple. The rest of us are likely to feel about it as St. Augustine did about Time. "I know what it is," he said, "until you ask me." The interlocutors in Dryden's *Essay of Dramatic Poesy,* after observing that "neither Aristotle nor Horace nor any other" had ever given a definition of a play, settle upon the following one:

A just and lively image of human nature, representing its passions and humours, and the changes of fortune to which it is subject, for the delight and instruction of mankind.

But this clearly won't do. Since it says nothing of the theatre or acting, why should it not also apply to the novel or the short story or even lyric poetry? Indeed, since it says nothing of the artistic medium, might it not even apply to the non-literary arts—painting, sculpture, ballet, what-not?

Dictionaries do rather better. "A composition in verse or prose, depicting life or character by means of dialogue and action, designed for performance in the theatre." Thus says the first one I have happened to pick up, and we must admit that it does rather better than Dryden and his friends. But dictionaries, as their name implies, are much more concerned with giving you the meaning of a word than with stating the nature of a thing; their definitions are usually circular, and carry you through a greater or smaller circle of words in the hope that you will know the meaning of one of them and so be satisfied. A cheap vest-pocket dictionary can settle the matter with a very small circle indeed: *"Play:* A drama. *Drama:* A play."

7

I am fussing about in this way, not because I intend immediately to offer a definition of my own, and so satisfy a long-felt human need, but because I should like to avoid a definition so hard and flat and final that it will preclude the possibility of a play's being something *other* than the thing defined. I want, in other words, to avoid too narrow a notion. That was the trouble in the *Agamemnon* class. If, for instance, you take the dictionary definition quite seriously (and it seems ever so trustworthy and deserving of being taken seriously, doesn't it?) you find yourself at once in the odd position of having to maintain that radio and television plays are not plays, for they are obviously "not designed for performance in the theatre." Incidentally, you find yourself simultaneously obliged to admit that any piece of vaudeville patter is a play, for it complies with all the conditions of the definition. That, however, is a minor matter beside the first. In the arts it is the too narrow notion, rather than the too broad, which will hurt you. When you exclude something, you are likely to find that you have only excluded yourself from it. Decide that the Nō plays, for example, are not real drama, and you simply cut yourself off from appreciation of the very real dramatic qualities of the Nō.

Narrowness is bad; worse still is false emphasis in definition. "A play is a literary composition in verse or prose . . ." No, a thousand times no. A play is *not* a literary composition. It is something which *may involve* literary composition, and that is a very different thing. A good play remains a good play even in translation, as long as the translation is not too inadequate;

8

and no amount of style-polishing will turn a bad play into a good one. The greater part, and the chief part, of playwriting has nothing to do with words; and the dramatist who fails to realize this is in for some disappointment.

What is a play if it is not a literary composition? We shall be better able to see what it is, I think, if we defer the whole business of definition and examine the conditions which make drama possible. I suppose that everyone would agree that a universal and absolute condition of drama is the possibility of its being *enacted.* That is, whatever a play is, it is something that can be acted out; if it cannot, it cannot be a play; and if acting were impossible, drama would be impossible. Perhaps there is room for a little cavilling here, but nothing that we need take very seriously. It is true that beginning playwrights sometimes produce "plays" that cannot be acted, but these are plays in intention only. And there is, of course, the matter of closet-drama. I do not agree with a student of mine who once defined it as drama which should be put in the closet and kept there; I will merely say that it seems to me to use dramatic devices for other than dramatic ends, and thus to lay no claim upon our consideration here.

So a play is capable of being acted out. But what do we mean by *acting,* and what are the conditions upon which acting depends? The first condition of acting is clearly impersonation, in the etymological sense of the word. Impersonation: assuming the mask, the guise, of something else. It may include a good deal more than the pretense of one person that he is someone

9

else. It may include human beings pretending to be animals, as in Rostand's *Chantecler,* or dressed-up sticks of wood offering themselves as people or animals, as in puppet and marionette plays, or even such insubstantial things as shadows in the semblance of people or animals, as in the shadow-puppet plays which are popular in some parts of the Orient. It matters not: the idea is that something presents itself as something else.

Without impersonation there is no acting; but not all impersonation is acting. We may at once exclude ordinary hypocrisy and fraudulent impersonation, and learn something from that very exclusion. There is no real deception in dramatic impersonation. The audience is perfectly aware that the guise is a guise, that the pretended entity is pretended. In fact, the audience cannot respond appropriately unless it knows that the fiction is a fiction. There are innumerable jokes about bumpkins and simpletons who did not know that the actors were merely acting; you may remember the little comedy that Henry Fielding provides in *Tom Jones,* when Partridge takes the ghost in *Hamlet* for a real ghost. We laugh at such ignorance; the fact that we laugh demonstrates that everyone ought to know that the acting is not intended as deception.

But impersonation by itself, even when it is not intended to deceive, is not acting. An actor may come on stage in an assumed character and merely offer us a long narrative, in the manner of the Chorus in *Doctor Faustus* or of Gower in *Pericles, Prince of Tyre.* This is not acting. And acting involves more than wearing a costume, or everyone at a costume party would be an actor. It involves more than dramatic recitation; more than the striking of postures, as in living pictures or *tableaux;* more than posture, gesture, and motion, as in ballet-pantomime; and more than these even when they are coupled with facial expression, as in pantomime proper. Some of these are undoubtedly departments of acting, which use certain restricted means; but I think we must say that acting as a whole potentially involves the whole body of human activities to effect its representation.

And we must qualify even further. It makes a great deal of difference *what* is represented, and what it is represented *as,* and *how* it is represented. Charades are acted out, but the enacting represents, not an activity, but a word or part of a word. Religious rituals are enacted, but the enacting is understood as representing the literal or symbolic re-enactment of a supposedly real event. Again, when the Emperor Commodus assumed the role of gladiator and vanquished his opponents in the Roman arena, he was not quite acting. These fights were offered as real fights, whether they were believed to be such or not; and the Emperor's opponents, if they only pretended to fight, did not pretend to die.

Moreover, the actor does not engage in his activities for pleasure, as children do in their make-believe; or in order to acquire knowledge, like children "acting out" the orbits of earth, moon, and sun in the classroom; or in order to acquire skill, like salesmen acting out "sales situations" in schools of salesmanship. The actor acts in order to depict the activities of someone

11

or something he is impersonating, solely for the effect which this is to have upon an audience. The peculiarity of that effect is something we shall have to look into later.

So much for acting; now, a play is, very generally, the whole scheme of action which underlies a given piece of acting, defining what the actor shall do, and indicating—usually very particularly—what he shall say. Since the actor is imitating an action, it is obvious that a play is, first of all and essentially, an imitation of an action. In order to contrive such an imitation, the playwright himself must be an imitator, assuming the persons of the characters of his play and speaking as if he were they.

This is an excellent point to say something very obvious—even though I said it earlier—since it is constantly forgotten by professors of literature and even by serious dramatic critics. A play is not a literary composition; it is a *play*. It is in fact quite unlike other literature, even when it is literature. The poet, the novelist, and the short-story writer are simultaneously producer, director, actors, scene-designer, orchestra, and even a crew of critics, reviewers, psychiatrists, and what-not commenting upon the show whenever it is useful for them to do so. The dramatist is not. He can only request some articles of furniture and other properties, which he may not get; he can outline a general plan of action which directors and actors must make specific in performance, if there is to be a performance; and he can determine what the actors are to say, but not how they are to say it. A poem or a work of fiction is the product of a single art; a drama, when performed, is the product of a complex of arts.

Precisely because a performed drama arises out of a complex of arts—out of several arts in collaboration —the dramatist has only partial and imperfect control over the means which are to take him to his projected end. Poems and novels are complete in themselves. You cannot perform them; you can read them aloud, beautifully or badly; that is all. And it will not matter, so far as they are concerned, which you do, for it will always be evident what is attributable to the work and what is attributable to your reading. It will be easy, too, for anyone to check up on you by reading the piece afterward, for these works, however much they depend upon the sound of language, are designed to produce their effects upon a *reader*. The dramatist is in fact much closer to the composer or the choreographer than he is to other writers. He is the architect of a plan which will have to be realized by someone else, and which will have its full significance and effect only when it is so realized.

What is more, the audience will see and hear what the dramatist can only imagine. In every other literary art the writer devises something in his imagination which affects the imagination of the reader. Imagination addresses imagination. But the dramatist proposes to affect his audience through *sensation* first of all, and through imagination only secondarily. Is this a small point? By no means.

Impressions, as David Hume says, are more vivid than ideas. That is, anything you perceive through your senses is generally more vivid than anything you can imagine. You can test this statement immediately by

13

experiment. Look at any object around you, observe its color and shape; then close your eyes and imagine it. You will notice at once that the object imagined is far less distinct in shape, and far less vividly colored. If not, you are either a highly unusual human being, or someone in a highly unusual state.

Now try another experiment: instead of looking at a real object and subsequently imagining it, try the power of words to call up images in your imagination. In order to make this as fair as possible, let us take a few verbal images which are famous for their vividness:

> The barge she sat in, like a burnish'd throne,
> Burn'd on the water; the poop was beaten gold;
> Purple the sails, and so perfumed that
> The winds were lovesick with them; the oars were
>   silver,
> Which to the tune of flutes kept stroke, and made
> The water which they beat to follow faster,
> As amorous of their strokes. For her own person,
> It beggar'd all description: she did lie
> In her pavilion—cloth-of-gold of tissue—
> O'er-picturing that Venus where we see
> The fancy outwork nature; on each side her
> Stood pretty dimpled boys, like smiling Cupids,
> With divers-colour'd fans, whose wind did seem
> To glow the delicate cheeks which they did cool,
> And what they undid did.

A wonderful, wonderful passage. As people say, "You can just see the whole thing." But—*can* you? Can you really *see* it? In that case, what is the exact location of the barge? Which way is it facing? What is its exact

14

shape? Of what shape are the sails, and the oars? *Et cetera, et cetera.*

Try the same thing on these:

> 'Tis her breathing that
> Perfumes the chamber thus; the flame o' the taper
> Bows toward her, and would under-peep the lids
> To see the enclosed lights, now canopied,
> Under these windows, white and azure laced
> With blue of heaven's own tinct.

> On her left breast
> A mole cinque-spotted, like the crimson drops
> I' the bottom of a cowslip . . .

> The roof o' the chamber
> With golden cherubins is fretted; her andirons—
> I had forgot them—were two winking Cupids
> Of silver, each on one foot standing, nicely
> Depending on their brands.

Do not protest that the kinds of detailed questions I am requesting you to ask are perfectly irrelevant to Shakespeare's purpose. I admit that. And do not tell me that here words do all that words can do to build clear and powerful images in the imagination. I admit that, too; in fact I chose these passages for that very reason. All that is beside the point. The point is that, clear, vivid, and precise as these images are, they do not and cannot have the clarity, vividness, and precision of things actually perceived by sensation. They can do a great deal more for you than the actual witnessing of the scenes might have; but they also do a great deal less. A hundred thousand artists, instructed

15

to draw an actual scene from exactly the same position and to draw exactly what they saw, would produce very similar pictures; instructed to draw what is described in the passages above, they would produce pictures no two of which would be alike. The imagination can build only very generally, give only very relative notions of position, shape, color, and so on. Sensation is precise.

Very well, you may say, what of it? Does it matter? It matters very much indeed. It matters so much that you cannot tell, simply by reading a play, whether it is good or bad *as a play*. Good plays sometimes read poorly; bad plays sometimes read well. So important is this distinction between the actually sensed and the merely imagined, that failure to recognize it is almost bound to produce a dramatic failure. Ignored, it makes drama seem a subdivision of some other literary form. The novelist who thinks of drama as a mere department of fiction and the poet who thinks of it as a mere department of poetry are headed for certain failure as dramatists, even when the novelist has the gift for the sensational that Robert Louis Stevenson had, or when the poet has the "dramatic" flair of Robert Browning.

Why should the difference between the sensed and the imagined have such importance? Well, in the first place, things which we actually witness affect us differently, in both kind and degree, from things which we merely imagine. What is terrible when imagined may be ridiculous when seen: Achilles' pursuit of Hector round and round the walls of Troy is horrifying in the *Iliad*, but it would be laughable on the stage. We read daily, with relative indifference, of events which would have filled us with emotion, had we seen them. We can be strongly moved by a vivid description of a certain event, but not so strongly as we should have been moved by witnessing it. We can hear of a typhoon in Japan which has killed thousands, and continue with our breakfast; but we can see a cat killed by a car and have the incident ruin our whole day.

Let us grant that the imagined may approach the witnessed in vividness; that the fully and vividly imagined may even in certain circumstances produce a more powerful effect than something witnessed; that the dramatist must sometimes call upon our imagination rather than appeal to our senses; and any other exceptions of the sort. The fact still remains—made more obvious by these very exceptions—that what is witnessed produces effects different from those arising out of the merely imagined.

There is another important consideration. Things which are credible when imagined are sometimes incredible when seen, and what is credible when seen may be incredible when imagined. An absolute impossibility may pass unnoticed when we read. I wonder how many persons have noticed, for instance, that in *Treasure Island* Billy Bones falls face-foremost to the floor, and that a few pages later, though he is dead and no one has moved him, he is lying on his back. This would hardly go unnoticed on the stage. Conversely, the limited resources of even the best equipped stage may make incredible an event which the imagination would accept without question. Indeed, the mere fact that something is presented on the stage may make difficulties. In life or in fiction we should not ordinarily trouble too much about whether—for example—a flag streamed in the wind or hung limp at the staff. But in *Little Eyolf,* as William Archer tells us, a flag offers some possibilities of embarrassment. If it is allowed to hang limp, it mutely declares the stage to be nothing but a stage; if it is set streaming by a fan, it sets the audience wondering about the mechanism which moves it. In either case it takes on an emphasis far beyond its dramatic importance.

All of these considerations push us toward the conclusion that there are important differences between an action which is suited to narration and one which is suited to dramatic presentation. What, then, is a dramatic action? We shall have to be very careful here. The drama of one culture is likely to seem "undramatic" to audiences of another. Occidental audiences may object to Oriental plays, or English audiences to French plays, or modern audiences to ancient plays. All this stems from the same kind of trouble that my old class had with the *Agamemnon;* that is, from an entirely too narrow view of what drama is and can be. We shall want to escape such provincialism, if we can; at the same time, we must not broaden our view to the point where anything and everything is "dramatic." Quite clearly, certain actions are more effective when acted, and others when narrated.

I think that everything we have discovered about acting in some manner applies here. Now, acting is a matter of the *external* behavior of the actors, since that is all that the audience can in fact witness; thus it appears that a dramatic action is one the important parts of which can be set before us most effectively through the visible and audible behavior of the characters.

We come to know about characters in drama much as we come to know about persons in daily life. There are three ways in which we come to such knowledge: either we witness something directly, as, let us say, we know that Jones beats his wife because we see him doing it; or we infer it from what we observe, as we might from the fact that Mrs. Jones is seldom without a black eye; or we are told about it, by the Joneses themselves or by someone else. Everyone has an outer obvious life and a secret inner life. In the real world, we know the inner life of others chiefly from what we can observe or find out about the outer; in drama we are almost wholly dependent upon the observed outer life for information about the inner. In the real world our ignorance of the inner life of others may be lessened by an occasional confession; in drama, by an occasional soliloquy; but certainly E. M. Forster is right in saying that the inner life of other human beings can be fully known only in the novel and other narrative forms. It is thus obvious at once that two kinds of actions can never be dramatic: those in which the outward behavior of the characters is inconsistent with their inner condition, and those in which the outward behavior requires constant explanation and comment in order to be understood. I pass over a kind which is even more obviously undramatic: actions involving inner conditions which eventuate in no outward behavior whatsoever.

Conversely, a dramatic action is one which can be

19

represented, directly or indirectly, by external behavior. Any kind of *physical* action can be represented directly; that is, by the actor's performing, in reality or in seeming, the very act itself, such as putting on a kettle, kissing the heroine, and so on. But inner and private conditions—except when a character simply tells us what is going on inside him—can be set before us only indirectly: that is, through outward signs from which we can infer them. In common phrase we say, "I see that you are angry" (or ill or brave or whatever); in fact we see only the outward signs of these conditions.

These signs are so important—comprising, as they do, not merely the chief part of excellent acting but also of excellent play-writing—that we must dwell on them for a moment. Suppose that they did not exist or that we could not infer from them. The effect on human life in general would be incredible, but let us consider drama merely. In the first place, only physical activity could then be represented on the stage; we should have plots only of external incidents, such as we have in the poorest Westerns and adventure programs on television: incidents which we should have to take at face value, in their most superficial aspects. The actor could *tell* us that he was angry, brave, sick, and so on; but he could never speak or act *as if* he were. The powerful effects produced on us by the manifestation of grief, joy, love, hatred would now become impossible; so also would be the exhibition of the deeper issues which underlie human actions; indeed, since a very great part—and probably the most important part—of human activity is psychic, taking

20

place within the human soul, it is clear that we should be condemned to very incomplete depictions of human life itself. The audience could see humanity only as the most superficial, unobservant, insensitive, and unsympathetic spectator might view it; and the dramatist, however profound his understanding of mankind and however great his genius, could produce nothing but unfeeling and inconsequential trash.

What are these signs upon which drama so heavily depends for its lifelikeness, its vividness, its emotional power, even its significance? They fall, on consideration, into two classes, the natural and the artificial. In our present concern, natural signs are always the effects which manifest a given internal condition as their cause. Thus a pale and haggard face, tears, a faltering voice, and so on, are signs of grief, since grief naturally produces such effects; emotions, desires, temperaments, dispositions, physical conditions and feelings, thoughts, moral character—in short, all the phenomena of the inner life—produce characteristic effects which function as signs from which their causes can be inferred. Artificial signs, however, are not causally related in this fashion; they always depend upon some convention or agreement which must be known if anything is to be inferred from them. They are either societal in origin, or are established as a convention of a particular kind of drama, or established within a given play itself; thus funeral wreaths or black armbands are conventional signs of mourning in certain societies, the passing of the hand before the eyes is a conventional sign of deep grief in Nō drama, and Dr. Rank's calling-card with the black cross over the name is established within *A Doll's House* as a sign that he considers his death imminent. Natural and artificial signs produce the same *kind* of effect upon us, since they permit us to infer exactly the same conditions; they differ however in the *degree* of that effect, for the natural sign is usually much the more powerful, as more immediately connected with the condition. For example, if you have a friend with a sick wife, you feel the same emotion when you see crape upon his door as when you see the man himself exhibiting his grief; but you are more deeply moved by the latter.

Realistic acting primarily employs natural and societal signs, together with direct representation, that is, the real or apparent doing of the action. Since natural signs are the same everywhere (Chinese groaning or weeping is no different from Spanish groaning or weeping, and means the same thing) and since an action is also everywhere the same (a Chinese kindling a fire is understood as doing so by a Spaniard), it is obvious that such acting is universally intelligible, except possibly in its societal signs. Certain highly formalized kinds of drama, however, such as the Nō, represent not merely internal conditions but also external action by artificial signs which are peculiar to the dramatic form itself, and consequently approach the esoteric. If you do not happen to know that carrying a spray of bamboo-grass betokens insanity, or that one motion with a fan represents drinking from a cup, another motion with it represents beating with a stick, and yet another loosing an arrow from a bow, you are likely to have some trouble in interpreting the action and consequently in responding appropriately to the drama. Was someone killed, and shall you be upset? Did someone have tea, and shall you be pleased? Or was someone beaten, and if so, is it too bad or very funny? Or is someone simply hot? Is the lady with the bamboo-grass doing a little gardening? Or flower-arranging? Or brushing off flies? Unless you are so delighted with the masks and costumes and the music and dancing—as you may very well be—that you aren't bothered, you may be very puzzled indeed; and unfortunately human puzzlement often terminates in ridicule or exasperation.

But we must worry a little more about this matter of signs. A dramatic action is one that can be acted out, and chiefly through external signs. It is only reasonable, therefore, that the conception of dramatic action should be greatly affected by the kinds of signs generally employed, much as it makes some difference whether a play is written for a box-set or "picture-frame" stage, an apron stage, or theatre-in-the-round. And this is in fact the case. An audience used to acting which employs one kind of sign is likely to have a quite different notion of "dramatic action" from an audience accustomed to acting which employs another kind. For one thing, different kinds of signs offer different possibilities of representation. Some things cannot really or apparently be done; you cannot, for example, really or apparently make a long journey on the stage, you can only offer some token performance of it. There are many internal conditions or experiences which are not manifested by any distinctive natural sign. When Henry James demanded that the actors in his play "simply look as if they had just had tea," without putting down tea-cups or using napkins or anything of the sort, he was demanding an impossibility of naturalistic actors. A novelist may easily say, "They had the relaxed and complacent look of persons who have just come from tea," but a dramatist depending upon natural signs must recognize that people who have just had tea do not have a look which differentiates them from those who have had other meals, or other experiences which might make them relaxed and complacent.

What is impossible through natural signs is, however, often possible through artificial signs. If a stone can signify the world, an actor can walk around the world in a moment; if a lamp can signify the sun, he can journey from the earth to the sun and back in a breath. If holding a fan in a certain way can mean that you have just had tea, you can have the look of someone who has just had tea. What limits you here is not the possibility of simulating the thing represented, but the existence of the artificial sign, or the possibility of establishing such a sign.

Occidental drama has from its origins relied mainly upon the use of direct representation and natural signs; drama which most of us think of as characteristically Oriental has relied mainly upon artificial signs which have been conventionally established. Even Western fantasy—*Peter Pan* and *Dear Brutus,* for example—is commonly intended for realistic acting. On the other hand, even historical actions are depicted through artificial conventions in Nō.

Once you commit yourself to direct representation

and natural signs you commit yourself to some degree
of verisimilitude, lifelikeness, convincingness, or whatever you wish to call it—at any rate, to some definite
approximation of the enactment to the thing enacted.
The action of a character putting on a kettle will have
to be depicted by an actor who goes through the appropriate motions which will have to take the appropriate time and be performed in an appropriate
place upon appropriate objects, and so on. Carry such
literalism far enough, and you will wind up with some
extremely restricted ideas as to what stage action can
represent. It is no accident that Western Neo-Classical
criticism should have developed the doctrine of the
Three Unities of Time, Place, and Action. If you take
the naturalistic view, how can the brief period of stage
performance be reasonably supposed to represent much
more than the events of a single day? And how can
the stage, once supposed to be a given place, presently
come to represent another, in one and the same play?
Preposterous, preposterous! You are even likely to conclude with Neander in Dryden's *Essay,* that it is a
very great beauty in a play to have the time of performance exactly equal to the time of the depicted
action; you are likely to conclude, too, with Dryden's
Lisideius, that death cannot be represented upon the
stage since the actor does not in reality die. Such doctrines as these seem to me to be founded not so much
upon critical theories and specific lines of argument as
upon the general concept of dramatic action which
underlies both theory and argument, and makes them
acceptable. So far as I know, the Three Unities have
today only a single exponent, and a somewhat half-

hearted one—T. S. Eliot; but the conception of dramatic action as essentially realistic still produces consequences which, if different from the Three Unities, are equally stringent. To give one single example: the modern notion, very widely current, that dramatic dialog must be modelled upon ordinary speech.

There is another aspect of the Occidental view of dramatic action which we must take into account. It is, I believe, an immediate consequence of the one we have just been considering. If you hold that the enactment must approximate the actual action depicted, the enactment can derive its interest only from the intrinsic interest of the depicted action. That action, then, must be one which is intensely interesting and exciting in itself. This notion of the "dramatic" has left its mark on our language; we say that an event, a personality, or even a room is "dramatic," to connote some special interest and emotional effectiveness. So far as the drama itself is concerned I do not think we should consider an action which involved no human crisis, whether serious or comic, an appropriate action for a play. The emphasis upon emotional intensity has been present in Western criticism from the first. For example, in the *Republic,* Plato makes Socrates remark that poets address the passionate and changeful element in the soul, and that the best of us are rapturous over the poet who can arouse our emotions most profoundly; in the *Poetics,* Aristotle grounds his preference for the complex plot upon its ability to produce the tragic emotions to the greatest degree.

I am not arguing that there is anything wrong with

26

these views of dramatic action; I am simply saying that they are not the only possible view. It is obviously possible to take an action of no great emotional potency and to depict it through conventional artificial signs (which, as I have said, are less forcible than the natural) and yet produce drama of the very highest order; and it is obviously possible simply because it has been done, time and time again, in the Nō plays and similar drama. Such drama is not likely to arouse violent emotion, nor is it intended to; it is intended to convey a sense of beauty, serenity, elegance, and subtlety, and in that intention it is perfectly successful. I should not wish to see Western dramatists drop what they are doing and imitate the Nō; but perhaps we might broaden a little our notion of what makes for dramatic action.

Are there any other characteristics of dramatic action, besides those we have noted? There are a few things, I believe, but I want to propose them with a certain diffidence. In the first place, the action of drama tends to be chiefly interpersonal. It is action, that is, which is not confined to the purely private sphere, as is so often the case in lyric poetry; it is in the main something done by someone to someone else, of such a nature as to affect his condition or fortune. In a word, it is action in which people act upon each other. Even when the play is restricted to a single actor, as in Cocteau's one-act monolog, *La Voix Humaine*, the action is still action between persons.

And of course, the action must be one of a certain length or extension. That extension will vary with different kinds of plays, but clearly there is a limit. I do not think the *Quem Quaeritis* trope a play, even though it is usually designated as the beginning of modern European drama, and though it was unquestionably performed. It consists only of three very brief speeches:

ANGELS: Whom seek ye in the sepulcher, O followers of Christ?

THE MARYS: Jesus of Nazareth, who was crucified, O celestial ones.

ANGELS: He is not here; he is risen, as he foretold.

Go, announce that he is risen from the sepulcher.

Finally, we may also say, I think, that it must be primary and comprehensive. Nothing can really be called a play, in which the action is merely incidental to declamations, songs, dances, and so on. The action must be primary, at least in the sense that everything else arises out of it, so that it comprehends them and is not itself comprehended in them.

But perhaps we have already begun to narrow our notion too much. Suppose we simply bear these things in mind as we explore further.

II
The Elements of Drama: Plot

POETRY AND FICTION of one sort or another seem to have existed in almost every kind of society, from the most primitive to the most cultivated, and in almost every period. You would, I think, find it somewhat difficult offhand to indicate any very extensive period of which you could say positively that neither existed anywhere. I prefer to ignore Horace's "Many unwept and unknown are swept into eternal night, because they lack the sacred bard," together with Alexander Pope's paraphrase of it, "They had no poet, and are dead." This proves nothing: the sacred bard, with all his huge literary luggage, may also have been swept into oblivion, for all we know. Like poetry and fiction, music, dancing, painting, and sculpture seem to have flourished practically at all times and among all peoples. The case of drama is different. Drama generally develops late, as compared with other arts. A complex art requires the fulfillment of many conditions before it can exist, and of many more before it can develop significantly. Some of these conditions cannot possibly be fulfilled in certain societies, and in consequence drama does not exist in them or reach any significant development. Great dramatic periods themselves seem to be brief.

Despite all this, there is an enormous mass of what we call dramatic literature—so enormous and so varied that you may well wonder how to deal with it. Suppose I ask you: How many forms of drama are there? You are likely to answer in one of two opposed ways, according as you are a Lumper or Splitter. These are not my terms, but terms which a biologist friend of mine tells me are in use, nowadays, among biologists quarrelling over problems of classification. A Lumper lumps everything into the same classes, to get as few classes as possible. As the Splitters put it, a Lumper sees a flying fish, a flying squirrel, a pterodactyl, a bee, and a duck, and lumps them all under *Bird*. A Splitter splits until there are as many classes almost as individuals: as the Lumpers put it, if a Splitter sees a sparrow with one feather missing, he wants to call it a new species. Polonius seems to have been a Splitter: you remember his famous "tragedy, comedy, history, pastoral, pastoral-comical, historical-pastoral, tragical-historical, tragical-comical-historical-pastoral, scene individable or poem unlimited," which continues to bring such glee and comfort to the hearts of Lumpers.

The difficulty with the position of the Lumpers is obvious. If you take the view of a late distinguished playwright and critic (who was a Lumper) that comedy is comedy, whether written by Aristophanes or Shakespeare or Molière or Goldoni or Shaw, you not merely ignore the development of different species out of primitive ones, but also ignore any development within a given species. What is worse, you force yourself to talk in such general terms that you can discuss nothing specifically. But it would be wise, also, to consider before you embrace the position of the Splitters. A Splitter cannot really deal with developments either, for he cannot find enough continuity to do so; he can only find a succession of mere differences. What is worse, lost as he is in a wilderness of apparently infinite forms, he finds it impossible to say anything about drama in general.

The Lumper can see nothing but resemblance; the Splitter, nothing but difference. Fortunately for the discussion of drama, these are both incomplete discussions, therefore; for the fact is that dramas both resemble one another and differ from one another. When we discuss anything completely, we discuss *all* of its characteristics; a play has individual characteristics, specific characteristics, characteristics which it shares with other forms of drama, and so on; even characteristics which it shares with every other kind of existence.

Even if the forms of drama were infinite or indefinitely numerous, however, it would still be possible to reduce them to their elements and to discuss these. No matter how great the complexity of structures, in their full proliferation and development, they cannot have generated out of infinite elements. If the *elements* of a structure were infinite in number, no such structure could ever have existed; for nothing can result from an infinite process such as would be required to assemble infinitely numerous elements. On the other hand, where elements are finite in number, it is always possible to discuss through them—that is, their number, nature, different possibilities of assembly and correlation and so on—the structures even of great complexity into which they combine. In fact, in this fashion physics and chemistry find it possible to discuss the fabric of the whole universe and everything within it.

Very well, then: What are the elements of drama?

I do not want to do what it is customary to do at the posing of this question: flourish my Aristotle and intone, Why, of course, Plot, Character, Thought, Diction, Music, and Spectacle. In the first place, these are not the elements of drama as such, but the specific parts of tragedy, derived in fact from the definition of tragedy. In the second place, not one of these terms means in Aristotle what it is likely to mean to a modern reader, and they are likely to be entirely misleading. I pass over the fact that their interpretation is a matter of some considerable controversy, has been so indeed for centuries, and that the debate is still far from being settled.

For the sake of simplicity and clarity I prefer to put the whole thing another way. If we think about the things a dramatist must do, as a *minimum,* to make a play, it becomes clear that he must (1) devise some sort of action, together with characters who can appropriately carry it out, (2) contrive a scenario which shows what actions are to be enacted on the stage in what order, and (3) compose the dialog, or at least indicate roughly what sort of thing shall be said by the actors. It appears that no play is possible without these three things; and that, on the other hand, the moment these three are completed, a play—good, bad, or indifferent, but a *play*—results. It is true that stage directions might be furnished, music composed, scenery designed, and so on; but these seem mere superadditions, ornaments and enhancements which are inessential to drama since drama can exist without them. Not a given *form* of drama, perhaps, such as Greek tragedy, Nō, or opera; but certainly drama.

These three things, then—action, scenario, and dialog—seem to be closely related to the elements of drama; and whatever ultimate constituents or parts these may divide into are in all probability the elements themselves, the ultimate particles out of which everything in the universe of drama is created.

We generally speak of the action of drama as *plot:* unfortunately, however, we tend to use that term in a variety of senses, some of them less accurate, or at any rate less useful, than others. Perhaps it would be wise to look into these before we do anything further.

The most general meaning of *plot* is that of the argument, synopsis, or summary of a narrative or drama. In this sense you tell someone the "plot" of a movie. The fact that you are frequently surprised and disappointed by your listener's reaction shows that your synopsis is not really the "plot" devised by the dramatist. Had your listener seen the movie himself, his reaction would have been similar to yours, in all probability. A synopsis or summary never precludes the possibility of opposite emotional effects; a plot is always aimed at some definite effect. A synopsis of the Pyramus and Thisbe play in *A Midsummer Night's Dream* is closely similar to a synopsis of *Romeo and*

Juliet. In both plays we have "two star-crossed lovers," parents averse to their union, clandestine meetings, the lover killing himself on the mistaken supposition that his beloved is dead, but it would be absurd to say that these plays have the same *plot;* one is comic, the other tragic.

For the same reason, plot is not a system of bare events or incidents in complete abstraction from character. Birth, marriage, parenthood, poverty, riches, death—any event, as *mere* event—can produce any number of different effects upon us, and thus no determinate effect. The death of a tyrant can bring joy, the marriage of an innocent girl to a villain can bring sorrow, though we commonly think of death as a sorrowful and marriage as a joyful event.

We also apply the term *plot* to a myth, legend, or series of historical happenings. This, too, seems inaccurate usage. Sophocles, Seneca, Corneille, Dryden, Voltaire, Hofmannsthal, Gide, and Cocteau all composed plays about Oedipus; can we say with any accuracy that all of these plays have the same *plot?*

Again, plot hardly appears to be mere intrigue or "conflict," although post-Elizabethan theorists often made it synonymous with the former, and nineteenth-century theorists often equated it with the latter. There are many plots—that of Sophocles' *Oedipus Tyrannus,* for example—which involve no intrigue whatsoever; similarly, there are plots in which no conflict is involved. What basic conflict can we find in *Our Town?*

Finally—and this is a subtler matter—plot is not the dramatic representation, or what we have just called the *scenario.* Parts of the plot, indeed crucial and

34

central ones, may be omitted from the representation, that is, may occur off-stage; the murder of Duncan, the death of Lady Macbeth and of Macbeth himself are obviously important parts of the plot, but they are not shown on the stage. Conversely, events may be shown on the stage which form no part of the plot. For example, Act I Scene i of *Julius Caesar* is not a part of the plot. It has no effect whatsoever upon the train of consequences which make up the action; it is merely an expository scene, intended to exhibit the fickleness of the Roman rabble, and so establish the probability of important events which happen later.

Other considerations go to show the difference between plot and representation. The plot may begin before the representation, or after it, or simultaneously with it; similarly, the plot may end before or after or simultaneously with the ending of the representation. It would be wearisome, perhaps pedantic, to illustrate all of this: I may simply remark that the representation in *Hamlet* begins long before the plot, which has its initiating incident in the information which the Ghost gives to Hamlet; that of *King Lear* begins almost immediately before the initiating incident of the plot, which is Lear's questioning of his daughters; while the representation of *Oedipus Tyrannus* begins after the beginning of the plot.

Further, the incidents of the plot are *time-bound,* that is, must occur in a given chronological order, and are consequently not convertible. The incidents of the representation are not time-bound, and conversions of chronological order are common. The commonest instance is the flash-back; only a little less common is the successive representation of simultaneous events—the well-known "In the meantime" of the silent movies. There is even what we might call the "flash-ahead," such as the Prolog to *Marco Millions,* which depicts events twenty-three years *after* the events of Act I Scene i.

If the matter is still not clear, one further reflection should set it beyond all doubt: when the dramatist has completed his plot, he must still determine what he will show upon the stage, in what order, on what scale. The scenario or representation cannot possibly be devised until the corresponding parts of the plot have been invented, for the representation is *what repre-sents,* whereas the plot is *what is represented.* They are thus, obviously, distinct.

Both representation and plot are actions, and dramatic actions. But the representation is a "dramatic action" primarily, in the sense precisely which we discovered in Chapter I, whereas a plot is "dramatic" secondarily, in the sense that it admits of being set before us by the representation. In other words, *any* plot is a dramatic one—regardless of the "actability" or "stageability" of the incidents which comprise it— so long as a dramatic scenario can be contrived to imply it. It is, thus, secondarily dramatic, as contingent upon the possibility of devising a dramatic scenario or representation. Henry James failed as a dramatist, not because he could not contrive dramatic plots, but because he could not contrive dramatic scenarios. The great success of some of his plays, as re-worked by competent dramatists, establishes this beyond question.

If plot is evidently neither the representation nor any of the other things we have been considering, what is it? For simplicity's sake I shall define it first and argue the definition afterward. *Plot is a system of actions of a determinate moral quality.* I use the word "actions" in a very general sense, to include the inner workings of the soul as well as external actions. In this sense, any actualization of a capacity for thought, emotion, or action is to be considered as "action."

I say "system of actions" because it seems unlikely that anyone would ever consider a single action or incident as a plot. A single, absolutely simple and indivisible activity, such as we find in the simplest forms of imagistic poetry, has never been called "plot" by anyone, so far as I know. Indeed, I suppose a good many people will balk at the notion of a plot as containing two, perhaps even three or four, incidents only. I shall come back to that later; for the moment, I say "system" as implying an activity (1) divisible into at least two activities, and (2) made into a system by some unifying principle. In saying "*some* unifying principle," I mean of course to imply that there are different possible ones.

The matter of "actions of a determinate moral quality" threatens to give us a little trouble. I shall simply give you the reasoning which leads me to insist upon this. I assume, as I said before, that plot is always aimed at some specific effect; that it is absurd to say that a tragic and a comic version of one and the same story have identical plots. If we then respond differently—as in fact we do—to events which in general synopsis are identical, that difference of response must be due to the different particular presentations of the events. Now, if we feel different emotions at the sight of the fortunes or misfortunes of characters in a play, we are of course feeling pleasures or pains, for the emotions are forms of mental pleasures or pains. Why do we feel these pleasures or pains? Because what we are seeing is in accordance with or in opposition to our wishes for the characters. What leads us to wish good or bad fortune for characters whom we have never known, and whose fortunes or misfortunes could never conceivably affect our own? Because we favor some, and hold others in disfavor. Why should we hold in favor or disfavor absolutely fictitious persons who exist in absolute detachment from our own self-interest? I can find only one answer to this last question: We feel toward them, this way or that, upon precisely the same grounds on which we feel one way or another toward persons who have existed in remote periods of history, or who are otherwise absolutely detached from our advantage or disadvantage; that is, upon *grounds of moral approval or disapproval*. But an action which incurs moral approval or disapproval must itself be possessed of a certain moral quality; thus the foundation of emotional effectiveness in plot must clearly be moral, and plot itself is morally determinate action.

Certain objections offer themselves at once to this view. As I see them, they appear only for immediate dismissal. First: Why should not we simply say that all our emotional reactions in drama are based upon general human sympathy? This can mean one of two things: that we feel, emotion for emotion, precisely what the character is feeling, or that our reactions are based upon the general love of man for man. The latter is patently false, for drama is filled with characters toward whom we feel the extremest antipathy. The former is false, too. Time and again we feel emotions which are the very opposites of those felt by the character. For example, we do not share the wicked glee of the villain at the apparent success of his plan, nor do we share the calm confidence of the heroine as she moves among unsuspected dangers.

Well, then, cannot we simply say that we identify ourselves with the characters? This is another very widely held view, and it can also mean one of two things. It can mean that we absolutely "put ourselves into the shoes" of the characters, that is, imagine ourselves as them, or that we identify our own interests with theirs. Both again are false and contrary to fact. These may possibly be principles of certain schools of *acting;* they are positively not principles underlying the reactions of the *audience.* Do we, in fact, in watching a play, fancy ourselves now as Claudius, now as Gertrude, now as Hamlet, now Horatio, and now Polonius? Or identify our own interests with theirs? In that case we should view the outcome with very mixed emotions indeed. If we identify ourselves with some but not with others, on what grounds do we do so? For identification cannot itself then be the *principle* underlying our reactions: it requires something further to explain it. Do we, in fact, identify ourselves with *anybody?* Is it not rather manifestly the case that as we watch, absorbed in what we see, nothing is further from our thoughts than ourselves and our self-interest?

The fundamental fault in both of these views is that each assumes that we cannot be moved emotionally without reflection upon our self-interest, and that our attitudes towards others must consequently be based upon self-interest. Man does not happen to be so insensitive nor so self-concerned. I will leave the matter there; David Hume has beautifully argued the rest of the case for me; I will merely say that our feelings at a play are such feelings as we have, not for ourselves, but for others.

There is one other objection, which a very able British critic, Mr. John Holloway, has brought against my definition of plot as morally determinate action. This would apply, Mr. Holloway observes, to the crude plots of Saturday matinee movie-melodramas, and the naive "good-guy and bad-guy" reactions of the children who go to see them; if so, how can it also be the basis of the subtlest reactions to the greatest drama?

I must answer that, in the first place, the question is not one of good plots and bad plots, but of what is and is not plot. In the second place, a definition of plot must offer universal attributes of plot, ones common to the highest and to the lowest kinds. Mr. Holloway's objection, far from being a real one, seems to me rather to make for my case; I should be disturbed indeed if my definition did *not* cover the movie melodramas. Besides, the possibility of a crude moral attitude in no way precludes the possibility of a more subtle and refined one. On the contrary, the subtle is possible only if the crude—or basic—attitude has been established.

Very well, then, we have our definition of plot, and we must ask another question: In how many ways may plots differ from each other?

First of all, they can differ in magnitude, in the extension of the action. The magnitude of the action is a function of the number of situations and of the number of characters which it contains. We can thus distinguish four kinds of magnitudes:

(1) the activity of a single character in a single closed situation

(2) the activity of two or more characters in a single closed situation

(3) the activity of two or more characters in a series of situations centering about a single principal event

(4) the activity of two or more characters in a series of situations involving more than one principal event.

The action involving a single character in a single closed situation is not common in drama as the whole action of a play. It can form a scene in a play, certainly; but as a whole action it is commonly found in lyrics, of which it is perhaps the commonest form of all. By a "closed situation" I mean one in which there is no external intervention of any kind; the character is as it were hermetically sealed off from the rest of the world, so that his action, thought, or emotion runs its uninterrupted course from beginning to end. This is the kind of action you will find in Keats's "Ode to a Nightingale," Milton's "Lycidas," Yeats's "Sailing to Byzantium," and similar lyrics.

The action involving two or more persons in a single closed situation is one that permits of many more possible developments, and so it is frequently found in short plays, and sometimes even in rather extended ones, such as Sartre's *No Exit (Huis Clos)*. Even here, however, complication of the action can arise only out of the characters themselves, and not from external interruption or intervention. As a consequence, it is difficult to develop an extended action of this sort.

When external causes or agencies are combined with internal, however, the case is very different. If you have two characters in a given situation and can bring in a third who can change that situation, you can proceed indefinitely. The third may appear in person or may be represented only as the writer of a letter or someone invisible on the other end of the telephone; it does not matter. Whether or not he figures in the *Dramatis Personae,* he is still an agent in the drama; and it is obvious that as we multiply agents or agencies we multiply the possibilities of development and hence of extension.

The last two kinds of action, thus, as permitting external intervention, offer far greater possibilities of developing an action of some length. Suppose we call the action of situations centering about a principal event by the name of *episode,* and the one which centers about more than one principal event by the name of *grand plot.* They are clearly distinct: the action of the *Agamemnon* is an episode, with everything

42

centering about the murder of Agamemnon; whereas the action of *Macbeth* is a grand plot, for it is impossible to designate in it any one event about which everything else centers.

So far as magnitude or mere extension of plot is concerned, I can think of nothing which goes beyond grand plot. But there is a matter of thickness or thinness, so to speak, as well as length. This is the matter of the number of lines or threads of action involved in a plot. A line of action is a chain of cause and effect, separable at least in part from other such lines. Plots are either linear or polylinear. The plot of the *Agamemnon* is linear, as consisting of a single line of action. The plot of *Oedipus Tyrannus,* on the other hand, is polylinear, and you can easily distinguish such different threads as Oedipus' investigations, the events happening at Corinth, and so on. When lines of action are such as to have an independent interest and constitute a story in their own right, they are called subplots, by-plots, or under-plots. The actions of Fortinbras and of Laertes in *Hamlet* I should consider lines of action simply; similarly, the successive actions of Albany in *King Lear* are merely a line of action, although a very important one. On the other hand, the Gloucester story is an under- or sub-plot.

Lines of action, whether or not they are sub-plots, either converge or diverge or run parallel. If you diagram a plot and find two or more lines of action stemming from a single cause or incident, this is divergence. If you find chains of causation concurring in a single effect or situation, this is convergence. If they are wholly independent of each other, they are parallel.

Divergence is commonest at the beginning of an action, as permitting complication; convergence is commonest at the end, to achieve resolution. Threatened convergence is one way of obtaining suspense, when the convergence is such as to affect the outcome materially; sudden convergence is one way of obtaining surprise. In *King Lear,* for instance, Albany almost understands the true state of affairs at certain points, and since he has the power to put an end to the villainy, may help Lear's situation: his line threatens to converge with Lear's. The unexpected return of Lovewit in *The Alchemist* is an instance of sudden convergence.

When lines of action are not merely causally related, as producing complication or resolution, they serve to enhance the effect of the main line of action, either through resemblance to it or contrast with it. Thus a comic sub-plot in a serious play contrasts with the main plot, and conversely. There are other more subtle possibilities: the Fortinbras and Laertes lines in *Hamlet* both reflect the main lines as similars and contrast with it, for Fortinbras is like Hamlet a dispossessed prince, and Laertes is like Hamlet the son of a murdered father, and yet both act in sharp contrast to Hamlet. In the same manner the Gloucester line in *King Lear* is both similar and dissimilar to the main line.

You can see at once that this offers all sorts of possibilities. Plots can begin with a single incident which produces a divergence of lines which never meet again. In John Buchan's *A Gap in the Curtain,* five men, after participating in an experiment in prevision, work out their separate destinies. Plots can end in the convergence, in a single incident, of lines previously more or less independent, as in *The Bridge of San Luis Rey*. They can involve lines which converge and diverge repeatedly, like the lines of Henry and the Master in *The Master of Ballantrae*. They can have lines that start independently and converge halfway through, to diverge and become independent again, as in Barrie's *Dear Brutus;* they can diverge from a single incident, run parallel for awhile, and then converge in the denouement; and they can do many another thing besides, which you may work out on your own by drawing lines on paper in the form of hourglasses, diamonds, strings of diamonds, zigzags, and what-nots. You will only need to bear in mind that divergence is the stemming of separate lines from a single cause, while convergence is the coming together of lines in a single effect.

I want to move on to another aspect of plot: its unifying principle, the thing which makes it a system and a single system. This is one of the aspects of plot construction about which critics have been most dogmatic, and it is one of the things about which it is most dangerous to be dogmatic. To prevent dogmatism as much as we can, let us consider four plays and ask ourselves what makes the plot of each *one* plot. I choose *Macbeth, Our Town,* Schnitzler's *Reigen (La Ronde)*, and *Ghosts*.

The plot of *Macbeth* has the unity of a train of consequences. The train has a beginning, an initiating incident (the meeting with the Witches), and it has a terminating incident (the killing of Macbeth and the passage of the crown to Malcolm). Everything in between is in some way an effect of the beginning and a

45

cause of the end; the whole has the unity of a causal sequence. The plot of *Our Town* is quite different. There is a certain amount of causal relation, to be sure, but it is not terribly important, and it is not the unifying principle of the plot. The plot is intended to catch an image of life in a small American town, and it is complete when it has caught that image completely, at least in its more nostalgic aspects. In this respect it resembles the plot of Dylan Thomas' *Under Milk Wood;* only it attempts to capture the image of town life through the three phases of youth, marriage, and death, whereas Thomas' plot attempts to reflect its image in the activities of a townful of people on a single day. This difference of organization is unimportant, however; the significant thing about this sort of plot is that it is complete in the sense in which a description is complete when it has adequately described its object. The incidents are present in it, not because they have any necessary causal relation, but because they show different aspects of the object in view. The plots of documentaries, chronicle plays, and many historical, biographical, and pageant pieces are of this order.

Schnitzler's *Reigen* has a different sort of plot again. The events are in no way causes or effects of each other, and they do not deal with any one object. They all deal with the theme of sexual love, but they are not intended to offer any very adequate description even of that. There are ten scenes: The Whore has sexual relations with the Soldier, the Soldier with the Parlormaid, the Parlormaid with the Young Gentleman, the Young Gentleman with the Young Wife, the Young Wife with the Husband, the Husband with the Little Miss, the Little Miss with the Poet, the Poet with the Actress, the Actress with the Count, and finally, the Count with the Whore. There you are: A and B, B and C, and so on, till we come full circle back to A. What sort of unity has this? Why, none, I say—unless you are willing to admit that a circle has unity or, more generally, that a pattern has unity. We can call this the *pattern plot*. Of course there are many possible patterns.

The plot of *Ghosts* is of still another kind. There is a causal sequence, but Ibsen is apparently so little concerned with it that he allows things to happen by convenient coincidence—for example, the outbreak of fire at a particular time—rather than go to the trouble of making them probable occurrences. It is hard to say what the initiating incident is. Is it the marriage of the Alvings? Or Mrs. Alving's flight from her husband? Or her return? Or his catching syphilis? Or the birth of Oswald? Or what? And what is the end? Does she poison Oswald or not? There are elements of the descriptive, too; but the unity of the plot is hardly that of a description. There is even a pattern of sorts; but that isn't primary either. The play is a *pièce à thèse;* the action and the characters are designed to prove, by example, that in a society in which duty is invariably opposed to pleasure, the good must suffer or become corrupt, while the wicked flourish in hypocrisy.

We have, thus, at least four different kinds of unifying principle in plots: the consequential, the descriptive, the pattern, and the didactic. I say, at *least* four; there may be many more.

47

We are likely to think that a plot cannot be complete unless it deals with a complete, and therefore finite, action. But in fact this applies only to the consequential plot. It is perfectly possible for a finite plot to convey the idea of an indefinitely continuing, perhaps eternal, process. There are a good many examples of this: *The Long Christmas Dinner, The Skin of Our Teeth,* and *Huis Clos* come to mind immediately. Some plots are complete when they afford an adequate basis for a certain emotion, some when they have made possible a certain inference. Some plots are stories; others, considered as stories, have no story at all, or are chronicles of very small beer indeed. What they do have in common is some end or other in view, and it is important to consider what that end may possibly be, for it is in terms of that and nothing else that the plot is complete.

To return to the question of other differences among plots: they can differ in terms of their laws of probability. This is a very difficult and complex question, and I can only deal lightly with it here. What I have in mind is that events which are probable or even inevitable in fantasy may very well be impossible in realistic drama, and that events which are probable or inevitable in farce may be impossible in ordinary comedy. The various forms of drama are in a sense different universes regulated by different laws, and the beings and objects within them operate according to those laws. We can distinguish several different systems of such laws or probabilities. We think an event probable if it happens daily or usually or frequently, to most people, or to most people at some time or other, or at any rate to people of a certain kind; and we think an action probable if everyone or most people or people of a certain kind have the power and the inclination to do it. This is common natural probability, and it is the kind of probability on which realistic and naturalistic plots are based.

We also think that rare and unusual occurrences are probable too, in certain circumstances, providing we believe that adequate causes exist, or that there are adequate indications that the occurrences happened. This is conditional natural probability, the probability of the unusual. Tragedy depends on it, and so does melodrama of the better sort.

We also accept as probable certain things of a highly exaggerated nature, because we recognize that the exaggeration, patently preposterous as it is, is only figurative and contains an element of truth. This is hyperbolical probability, and it underlies farce.

We even accept as probable the actions of beings we know do not exist, or actions which existent beings could not possibly perform, provided these follow upon a certain hypothesis. *If* witches, ghosts, and fairies existed, they *would* do such and such; *if* a dog could talk, he *would* talk like that. This is hypothetical probability, and it underlies all fantasy and stories of the supernatural.

We will accept anything as probable which corresponds to something already accepted. Thus a plot which follows a familiar legend or a familiar version of historical events will be accepted as probable, even though these latter contain improbabilities or impossibilities. No one will question the feats of Paul Bunyan,

49

or George Washington's cherry tree. This holds, too, of certain forms; for instance, we expect certain things to happen in a Western, improbable as they may be. This is the probability of custom, or conventional probability.

There is emotional probability, too. This may be completely irrational and in no way connected with logical probability. A given emotion predisposes us to believe certain things, even though they may be impossible. A man in a gloomy frame of mind finds it doubtful that anything good can happen; an audience in a certain emotional state will similarly accept things that in another it would question.

When I spoke earlier of "different universes regulated by different laws of probability," I did not mean to imply that these universes could not coincide, or at least impinge upon each other to some degree. They can, and often do. A plot of natural probability can turn to hypothetical probability (fantasy) and subsequently return to the natural: instances are *A Midsummer Night's Dream*, Dunsany's *If*, Barrie's *Dear Brutus*, and Shaw's *Man and Superman*. The natural probability can turn to the hyperbolical, as in Androcles' waltz with the lion in *Androcles and the Lion*. There are many other possibilities, one of the most fruitful of which seems to be the reversal of conventional probabilities; that is, the establishment of a different system of probabilities—within the framework of a legend or literary form—from those associated with that form or legend. This is one of Shaw's characteristic devices; he uses it in *Arms and the Man, Caesar and Cleopatra, Man and Superman, St. Joan,* and other plays. It has been used repeatedly also by Gide, Cocteau, Giraudoux, Sartre, and Anouilh to provide startlingly different versions of classical legend.

These shiftings of probabilities, or mixtures of them, seem to depend for their success upon a single principle; they must be required by the form, and themselves made probable within it. In *A Midsummer Night's Dream* separate lines are established at the outset, the human and the faery, each with its own probabilities. When the lines of action converge in the Wood, the natural and the hypothetical probabilities operate together; subsequently they draw apart again. The whole is probable because the convergence and the divergence have been made probable. In *St. Joan* an action which has been principally one of natural probability shifts, in the Epilog, into hypothetical. There has been much objection to the Epilog as "unnecessary," "improbable," and "destructive of the tragic effect"; I think these charges are very ill-founded. *St. Joan* is not tragedy, but a certain kind of comedy. As Shaw says, "The angels may weep at the murder, but the gods laugh at the murderers"; and he arranges matters so that Joan herself may have the last laugh— albeit a melancholy one. Her last laugh came with her canonization in the twentieth century, and so, if she is to enjoy the joke on her murderers, fantasy is required. The Epilog is essential to the play, for it contains the comic reversal; to delete it would be to alter the very form and significance of the play. This is a matter of the probability of form, and it underlies many of the great tragic denouements of Shakespeare.

If we consider probability in a different light, everything that is probable is so either intrinsically or through its connection with other things. In *St. Joan,* since we have been speaking of that, Shaw subverts the idea of the "miracles" as miraculous by supplanting them with events of intrinsic natural probability. The natural probability is always more probable intrinsically than any other. Normally we are more willing to believe that something is coincidence, or has been foolishly interpreted or knavishly misreported, than that it is actually miraculous. It would seem that this is the position of the Roman Catholic Church itself, since it submits all supposed miracles, I understand, to extremely rigorous tests.

On the other hand, extrinsic probability can very powerfully overcall intrinsic probability in some instances. Witch and fairy must do what witch and fairy would do, although both are impossible. Again, the spell of a particular emotion may be so powerful that under it we may doubt what we should normally believe, and believe what we should normally doubt.

There is probability even within the realm of accident and coincidence. That is, although we think of these as improbabilities, not all accidents are equally improbable. It is more probable that a car will collide with another than that it will be struck by a meteorite; that such-and-such will happen in the jungle than that it will happen in a city; and so on.

Plots of consecutive action are either simple or complex. A simple plot is one that moves in a single direction, as when the fortunes of the protagonist steadily decline or improve. A complex plot is one that involves a change of direction, as when the protagonist moves toward greater and greater good fortune, and then suffers reverses. A straight line and a bent line will give you the idea; the former is simple, the latter, complex. The complex is always divisible into distinct parts, while the simple is not: you can see that the bent line is made up of two discrete parts, but the straight line is continuous, and any point of division is arbitrary. The point at which the fortunes alter is the peripety or reversal. Discovery of some sort is usually associated with reversal, either as producing it or resulting from it. Someone learns that he has committed a dreadful mistake, or finds out in time to prevent it, and so on.

All complex plots involve at least two factors which we may call *force* and *counter-force*. The force is what carries the action initially in one direction; the counterforce is what produces the change of direction. Both must be probable, of course, as causes; but if the reversal is to be unexpected, the counter-force must be concealed, or made to seem improbable, while the force must be obvious and apparently irresistible. On the other hand, if the reversal is to be probable, the counter-force must be, in retrospect, far more probable than the force. The superiority of the complex plot lies in that it permits of the unexpected and hence of greater emotional power, since emotions that come upon us unexpectedly are always more violent and powerful.

Complex plots always involve complication, as their name suggests. There are two kinds of complication, the continuous and the incidental. The continuous operates from the first and throughout; the incidental operates only in a given part, is resolved and done with in that part, and another incidental complication must be introduced if further development is to result. The great Shakespearian tragedies involve continuous complication; Shaw chiefly uses the incidental. Thus in *Pygmalion* Doolittle appears, threatens to break up Liza's arrangement with Higgins, and withdraws. All momentary obstacles are of this order. Continuous complication depends primarily upon extrinsic probability, and incidental complication depends primarily upon intrinsic.

III
The Elements of Drama: Incident and Character

THUS FAR we have been talking about the length and thickness of plot-threads and how they can be twisted and interwoven—talking, as it suddenly seems to me, with touching innocence. True, there are certain questions which we cannot possibly handle at this point, such as why anyone should want to twist these threads, and why they should be twisted this way rather than that. But we have not said a word about what the threads are made of. What *are* they made of?

Incidents and actions, of course. Anyone knows that. In fact, we said as much repeatedly in our earlier discussion.

But what is *an* incident?

I have just been reading a historian who speaks of the Battle of the Bulge as "one of the crucial incidents" of the Rhine Campaign. So a whole battle is *an* incident. I am impressed by this grand view of things and spurred to try my hand at it. I succeed at once: "The Rhine Campaign was one of the crucial incidents of the Allied invasion of Europe." Can I do better? Of course. "The Allied invasion was one of the crucial incidents of World War II." Better still: "World War II was one of the crucial incidents in the international reorganization of modern Europe." As I continue in this grand way, more and more grandly, I recall the old bromide that if the age of the earth were a single day, all human history would be the last tick of the clock; all human history is an incident, then, and perhaps the word "crucial" is no longer necessary. And the existence of the earth is an incident in the history of the universe, and . . .

In the midst of my enjoyment of this godlike view, I remember a remark of Henry James's in *The Art of Fiction:*

It is an incident for a woman to stand up with her hand resting on a table and look at you in a certain way; or if it be not an incident I think it will be hard to say what it is.

I have no intention of undertaking something that struck Henry James as hard if not impossible. I concede: it is certainly an incident. Or rather, now that I look at it again, it is *three* incidents. She stood up, rested her hand upon the table, and looked at me. I should like to know more about that look; but I dismiss this curiosity in my astonishment that the scrupulous Henry James, even when he thought he was dealing with minutiae, should have mistaken three incidents for one. On second thought, *is* it one incident to stand up? Her feet would have to be placed upon the floor, her knees would have to straighten, and her hips, and . . .

You can see where this will carry us. An anatomist would see every one of these "incidents" as an enormous complex of incidents, and the more he knew about anatomy, the more complex they would become. If we forget about the physical movements, and concentrate only on the will which originates them (for I hope these are not involuntary movements), that apparently instantaneous mental action must divide, in the view of a psychologist, into another whole complex. It is enough to make you decide never to get out of bed again.

What is *an* incident? We have asked an apparently simple question and lodged ourselves in a metaphysical morass: the problem of what "an" or "one" means. Obviously every one of these incidents, from the most minute to the most enormous, is *one* incident. We can regard anything we care to as a unit in this way: a single body-cell, an organ of the body, a man, a company, a battalion, a division, an army, the whole mass of humanity, the universe. Of what *size,* then, are the incidents of which the novelist or dramatist is to build a plot?

Here is Tale 95 from the *Gesta Romanorum:*

We read in the Roman Annals of a certain tyrant called Maxentius, who would have deprived the Romans of their paternal estates. Yielding to the cruelty of the tyrant, they fled to Constantine, king of Britain.

At length, when many were assembled at his court, the emigrants stirred up the British monarch to revenge them upon the tyrant. Moved by their entreaties, Constantine mounted his horse, overthrew the tyrant, and restored the exiles to their inheritance.

This admirable tale moves me so that I must instantly write a play about it.

Act I

Scene: Rome

MAXENTIUS: Better give me your paternal estates. I'm very cruel.

ROMANS: He's very cruel. Let's give in.

(*They do, and flee to Britain.*)

Act II

Scene: British Court

CONSTANTINE: There are certainly a lot of you Romans here.

ROMANS: There certainly are. We want you to revenge us upon the cruel tyrant Maxentius, who has taken our estates.

CONSTANTINE: I won't.

Act III

Scene: The same

ROMANS: Please.

CONSTANTINE: All right.

Act IV

CONSTANTINE: Whoa, boy!

(*mounts horse and overthrows Maxentius.*)

Act V

Scene: Rome

CONSTANTINE: Here are your estates back.

ROMANS: Thanks.

I think everyone would agree that the incidents here are too small. A dramatic plot might contain *some* incidents of this size, like the capture of Don John at the end of *Much Ado About Nothing:*

> MESSENGER: My lord, your brother John is ta'en in flight,
> And brought with armed men back to Messina.

Obviously, however, a plot could not be composed wholly of such minutiae. On the other hand, here is the opposite extreme:

How did the centripetal remainer afford egress to the centrifugal departer?

By inserting the barrel of an arruginated male key in the whole of an unstable female lock, obtaining a purchase on the bow of the key and turning its wards from right to left, withdrawing a bolt from its staple, pulling inward spasmodically an obsolescent hinged door and revealing an aperture for free egress and free ingress.

This is James Joyce telling us of a nearly instantaneous event, the unlocking of a door. Evidently a plot could hardly consist of incidents of that size, either. These are not the ultimate extremes of bigness and smallness of incident; even so, no plot could consist wholly of incidents of either size.

Let us not hastily conclude that there is some kind of fixed mean between these extremes which gives us the proper size. A very little observation will assure us that incidents vary in size from work to work, and even within the same work. Not all the incidents in *Much Ado* are as small as Don John's capture and return under guard to Messina, and not all of the incidents in *Ulysses* are as extended as this unlocking of the door.

Let us notice something else. The narrative or dramatic incident is unlike the real incident in a very important respect. We can take indefinitely grander views of the Battle of the Bulge, until it ceases not merely to be crucial, but even to be an incident at all; and we can take indefinitely more minute views of a woman standing up—so long as this is a *real* incident —until that, too, ceases to be an incident because its moment has turned into a whole sequence. But this is what, in the fictitious incident, we positively cannot do. James is right: the woman rising, putting her hand on the table, and looking at you in a certain way *is* one single incident, if it functions altogether as a single indication of character. We can take grander or more minute views of the real incident and of its importance, because here the view is arbitrary; we take whatever view we please. But the view which we take of fictitious incidents is not arbitrary; the size of the incident, and its importance, too, have been determined for us by the writer, precisely because he has determined what view we are to take of them. An incident cannot be regarded as larger or smaller than the size actually given it by the writer. Unless he treats it as divisible, it is indivisible; unless he relates it to a larger context, it cannot be related to a larger context.

Further: in the little play I wrote, as in the narrative on which it was founded, the incidents are too small. Too small for what? Too small to have any effect—any effect whatsoever. The play is certainly ludicrous, but not as a consequence of the incidents as such; it is so simply because of the ineptitude it manifests, because of the absurdity of the notion that a play should be composed of incidents of such brevity. *Any* incidents, pathetic, fearful, ridiculous—whatever their emotional quality—would, if treated on the same scale, lose that quality to the same degree, and operate much as these do. We may conclude, thus, that the *proper* size of an incident is determined by the effect it is to have, or more specifically, by its function in producing that effect.

We must observe, too, that we are now talking of incidents in the *plot;* not incidents as represented in the scenario, or incidents as involving a greater or lesser amount of dialog. For I might extend the represented action indefinitely, and as long as I did not increase the number of incidents or the number of their constituent parts, the whole thing would remain as ineffective as before. For example, I can extend Act III to great length, by having each one of ten thousand Romans say, "Please," and having Constantine refuse all but the last; but while I will have immensely lengthened the scenario, I will not have affected the plot: the basic incident remains *one,* that of Constantine's acceding to their plea. In the same fashion, I can write extended speeches for each, instead of the simple "Please," but the incident of *plot* will remain unchanged. The only result of my efforts will be to demonstrate that there are questions of size or scale in the matter of representation and dialog as well as in plot.

But if an incident of plot can exist apart from its

61

representation and from any dialog, it can do so only as idea. How can we talk about the size of an idea? I can have the idea of a midge and an idea of a hippopotamus, together with the idea that one is certainly much larger than the other; but does it make any sense to say that *ideas themselves* are larger or smaller?

It would appear that we have landed in the realm of nonsense. But not quite. On second thought, we *can* measure ideas. Ideas can be simple or composite; and composite ideas can be more or less composite. They can divide immediately into their ultimate parts, or they can divide into parts which divide into other parts, and so on indefinitely. When you mention Paris in a list of cities, I hear you and respond with a simple idea; when you speak of the various *arrondissements* of Paris, and of the various streets and buildings within these, my idea grows more complex.

In the same fashion, the idea of an action can be simple, or it can be an idea comprising the ideas of many constituent actions, which can themselves contain the ideas of many constituent actions, and this indifferently as to the length or brevity of the action itself. In Tale 95, an Emperor can be overthrown in no more time than it takes to mount a horse; both are conceived in terms of equally simple ideas; but in Chapter XIV of Gibbon, the war of Constantine against Maxentius appears as a highly complex process which occupies many pages in the telling.

Again, if I remark that the news of the day includes a murder, a robbery, a fire, a suicide, a bank failure, and a divorce, you respond with simple ideas of these; but if I go into circumstantial detail you frame very complex ones. By "circumstances" I mean the doer of the action, the act, the purpose, the instrument with which it was done, the manner in which it was done, the person or object to which it was done, the result, the time, the place, and all similar matters.

It is, I think, unnecessary to show that we react with quite different emotions to a general idea of murder on the one hand and a highly circumstantial one on the other. What is more pertinent is to observe that, so far as the general or simple idea of murder is concerned, no one murder is more horrifying or exciting than another. At the same time we do not necessarily increase the interest or excitement of an event by going into all its circumstances, as any bore will be eager to demonstrate to you. The most horrifying murder in history must involve many circumstances that in no way make it more horrifying, that, indeed, may lessen the horror, or arouse other emotions to vie with horror, or arouse no emotion whatsoever. And a general circumstance may entail particular circumstances which either add to or lessen the emotional force of the incident. The murder occurred in a city, in a slum section of that city, in a church in that slum, in a church regarded as especially holy, at the altar of that church; these are all special circumstances of place, but some evoke more emotion than others. In the same way, if I divide an action into its constituent actions, the constituents may decrease or increase the emotional force of the action itself, for they themselves will be actions which arouse this emotion or that, to this or that degree, or be of no emotional force whatsoever.

If we are to give the proper size of the incident which is to evoke a given emotion, we may do so as follows: *the size which includes all the factors* (or *causes*) *requisite to produce the emotion in the desired degree.*

But incidents do not merely arouse emotion; they are probable or improbable, and cause other incidents to be probable or improbable. Some incidents are immediate consequences of others; but some are remote consequences, with many intervening incidents between them and their initiating cause. If I drop my watch, it will fall; the one incident is the immediate consequence of the other. But I matriculate in this school as a freshman, and obtain my doctorate seven years later, the graduation is a remote consequence of the matriculation. Where a process of any kind is involved, the probability of the final incident is dependent upon the probability of the completion of the process, and that probability is dependent upon the probability of the incidents involved in it: the chain is as strong as its weakest link. A widow in the midst of her grief promises to marry the man who has murdered her husband and father-in-law. Is that probable? Not as an immediate consequence; but as the result of a process of a special kind, under circumstances of a certain kind, it may be; and Shakespeare shows us the process and the circumstances in *Richard III*. A man makes a single speech and by it persuades a multitude to grieve for the death of a man whose murder has just brought them joy. Is that probable? Shakespeare shows us the process and the circumstances that make it probable in *Julius Caesar*.

A process, I think, involves two different kinds of things; conditions for the operations of causes, and causes themselves. If A is a sufficient cause to produce B, and B to produce C, and so on, the whole cause-effect chain goes off like a string of Chinese fire-crackers. If A requires certain conditions in order to produce B, and B certain others to produce C, these conditions themselves must occur, and perhaps these themselves may require yet other conditions, which must occur first. Our firecrackers go off successively because all of the conditions have been brought to exist: gunpowder and paper and glue and paper tubing and string have been made and assembled into the firecrackers, and the lighting of the fuse is a sufficient cause. The fulfilling of each condition is of course itself an incident, and itself must be inevitable, probable, or possible. Where any incident is probable "on the face of it," it can be conceived, so far as probability is concerned, as a simple idea. When it is not thus probable, that simple idea must be resolved into constituent factors until some are reached which *are* probable; that is, replaced by a composite idea containing the causes and conditions which make it probable.

Consider, for example, the fist-fight between the hero and the villain which serves as the dénouement of many Western movies. If the hero is the stronger and more expert, his victory is a foregone conclusion. Except for the excitement which attends almost any fight and the pleasure of seeing the right man win, the scene could well be omitted; the notion of stronger in combat with weaker produces the notion of victory for the stronger, and the script-writer can work in terms of general—that is, *simple*—ideas. But suppose the hero is weaker. Victory is now as improbable for him as it was probable before. He can win only if the villain is suddenly disabled, or if something happens to increase his own strength, or if some agency or other comes to his aid. The villain may be smitten with blindness, like Wolf Larsen in *The Sea Wolf,* or have a heart-attack, or become seized with panic, or stumble and plunge over the cliff; the hero may find some weapon, the noble horse or the faithful dog may come to his rescue. But these things cannot happen out of a clear sky; the constituent factors of the now composite idea of the fight will have to be probable in themselves or be made probable by some previous incident. The villain must be established as liable to blindness or panic; the weapon must be such as would probably come to hand; the aid must be such as horse or dog could probably give. What is more, just as there is this positive or promoting probability, there should be a negative or restraining probability, so that the event which turns the tables is unlikely until that particular point, *just then*. The horse is at some distance, the dog is straining at its tether, the hero never thinks of the weapon until his hand encounters it, the villain is secure until he brings on whatever disables him.

The incident, then, is to be of the right size or scale to give it probability. Here, as in the case of emotional power, the unskillful writer will usually do too

66

little or too much. You can give too little ground for emotion, or pile ground upon ground past the capacity of your audience to respond. You can fail to establish probability or over-establish it, and so produce incredulity or boredom. The right scale is a mean between these extremes; not an absolute one, but one relative to what the incident is to do, to what its function is.

Scale is determined by function, then. But the examination of all the particular functions of incidents would doubtless be a very long story. We can simplify this vastly if we consider the *general* functions of incidents.

I think we can distinguish four general functions. Two of these relate to the plot itself, and two to the representation. Any incident in the plot is either essential or factorial. In the plot of *Othello,* for example, the essential incidents are those which are involved in the working out of Iago's scheme to its tragic denouement. These are, in short, the major incidents of the plot. But there are many minor incidents which provide the necessary causal conditions for the major ones: these are factorial. For example, if Desdemona is to be smothered in bed, she must be there, and Othello must enter the bedchamber; murderer and victim must be brought together. I am distinguishing, I must remind you, not between incidents but between their functions: thus an essential incident may also have a factorial function, whereas a factorial one is factorial simply.

But a play also contains incidents which are not part of the plot, even though they are shown upon the stage. At least the greater part of Act I in *Othello*—perhaps all of it—is neither factorially nor essentially related to the plot proper. It is dramatic exposition in the form of action. It acquaints us with the general situation and with the characters, and disposes us to regard the latter in a certain light; but it is not part of the plot as such. This function of incident was so evident to critics of the sixteenth and seventeenth centuries that they spoke of such preliminary matter as the *protasis* of the play; indeed, high school texts still inform students that a play has three parts, exposition, complication, and resolution. In fact, however, exposition may occur at almost any point in the play, or be implied in the plot itself. For example, Hamlet's account of his voyage in Act V Scene ii is certainly expository, and in O'Casey's *A Pound on Demand* the plot explains itself as it unfolds.

Incidents of representation have two functions. They either make the plot or the representation itself more probable or effective; or they are ornamental purely. Thus Act I Scene i of *Coriolanus* is not part of the plot, for it leads to no direct consequence; like the first scene of *Julius Caesar* it merely establishes a condition for events that follow. Some incidents of representation are for the sake of the representation itself; for example, merely to effect continuity in it, as bridging-scenes and transitional passages. Finally, the ornamental incident is necessary neither to the plot nor to the representation; it is simply pleasurable or otherwise effective in itself. Thus the singing of the two songs at the end of *Love's Labour's Lost* is perfectly ornamental; the action has already been concluded, and this is simply a pleasurable addition. Songs, dances, parades, and so on, are usually ornamental. Not always, however: a song which discloses the identity of the speaker or causes someone to fall in love is obviously part of the plot, and the song at the end of Brendan Behan's *The Hostage* is more than ornamental, since the supposedly dead soldier springs up to join in it, and so discharges any melancholy we feel at his death.

We must bear in mind, through all of this, that a mental incident—a happening in the soul—is as much an incident as a physical incident. Plots differ as they are made up chiefly of one or of the other, or as they emphasize one or the other when they involve both. Thus a plot can consist almost wholly of physical incidents, as in the Westerns we seem to be mentioning so frequently; or it can consist almost wholly of mental events, as in the so-called "psychological" dramas; or it can consist of both, with emphasis chiefly upon one or the other. Shakespeare illustrates this last: his plays contain a good deal of physical action, but the emphasis is upon the mental event.

To this point we have been speaking as though all plots were plots of consecutive action. This of course is not the case, as we saw in Chapter II, and consequently it is possible that incidents in different plots have different kinds of functions. A little reflection informs us that this is more than a mere possibility; it is fact.

The plot of a descriptive drama, such as *Under Milk Wood* or *Life with Father,* is primarily a formula or description of its object, as we saw. It does not progress in the same manner as the consecutive action; such progress as there is depends upon gradual revelation or the development of emotion. The essential incidents are those which embody typical aspects or attributes of the object; in a sense, they are illustrative anecdotes in dramatic form. For example, if you are writing a play which is intended to capture the spirit of small-time carnival life, you must invent such characters as would be typically found in such a life, doing such things as would be typically done, so far as is consonant with the emotions you are trying to arouse. You are set free from the major problems which the play of consecutive action poses, so that you may show this or that facet of your object. Character can be expressed far more fully in incident, incident can be far more fully developed, since neither character nor incident is restricted by the necessity of advancing the action. The scale of the incident is determined by the nature and the importance of the attribute it depicts.

The incident of the pattern play is dominated by the pattern. It is used as a unit, and must be clearly recognizable as a unit; otherwise the pattern is lost. The incidents must therefore be of the same construction, be of about the same complexity, and have much the same length. The first incident pretty well determines the scale of the others. The pattern grows in one of two ways: either by a repetition of similar incidents which involve some point of difference, or by a succession of dissimilar incidents which nevertheless involve the same theme, or the workings of analogous causes, or some element, at any rate, in terms of which they are comparable. The incidents in *Reigen,* for instance, are similar, and those in *Pippa Passes* are dissimilar, except that each scene depicts a human crisis which is resolved for the better as Pippa's songs are overheard by the characters. In such plots, as in the descriptive ones, the unity of the plot is sometimes reinforced by some extrinsic natural unity, such as a day, the seasons of the year, a generation, and so on.

The incident in the didactic play must, from the nature of the case, function as an element of proof, and its scale, like its kind, must be determined accordingly. There are three kinds of didactic action because there are three kinds of proof: the inductive, the deductive, and the analogical. The inductive action exhibits examples from which we as audience are to generalize. Ibsen's didactic plays are generally of this nature; we are supposed, for instance, to generalize from the examples offered us in *Ghosts*. The deductive action offers generalizations which we are to apply to particulars: for example, *Everyman* is a dramatic embodiment of generalities; Everyman is not a supposedly particular person like Mrs. Alving. The analogical action always offers some fable or parable which is parallel or proportional to its thesis. The Fox is to the Grapes as the disappointed man to the object of his vain desire. Aesop's Fables or the parables of Jesus illustrate perfectly what I have in mind, and *Peer Gynt* is a dramatic example.

We must now consider incident in its relation to character, and there are important and difficult problems in connection with that relationship. One of these is posed by the very remark of Henry James's that we were contemplating a little while ago. The remark occurs in a passage arguing against the distinction of the novel of character from the novel of incident, and we had better look at it in context:

. . . What is character but the determination of incident? What is incident but the illustration of character? What is either a picture or a novel that is *not* of character? It is an incident for a woman to stand up with her hand resting on a table and look at you in a certain way; or if it be not an incident I think it will be hard to say what it is. At the same time it is an expression of character.

James seems to be saying three things: (1) that there is no incident which does not characterize, (2) that there is no character except as expressed in incident, and (3) that character is the more important of the two, despite this apparently reciprocal relation, since incident is determined by it.

James is speaking of fiction rather than drama, but I am not sure that in this case the differences between fiction and drama matter much, for incident is common to both. In any case, the first proposition, that there is no incident which does not characterize, is clearly false in point of fact. Obviously there are many things which happen both in life and in its fictitious counterpart which have no relation to character whatsoever, since they do not happen as a consequence of character, and would happen anyway, regardless of the kind of character involved. The eruption of a volcano, a thunderstorm, a plane or a train wreck, are certainly incidents; but some of these can have nothing to do with character, and others may or may not

72

have to do with it. Chance, nature, and compulsion are causes which can importantly affect whatever occurs, and whatever is due to these cannot be called a matter of character, since it is not even a matter of human agency. What is more, not even everything due to human agency can be called a matter of character. Many actions are performed by all men, regardless of differences of disposition and moral character itself. Even in fictitious action, I do not think we can say that Macbeth's simply meeting the Witches, or Banquo's taking the journey and being killed on his return, and a host of similar things, are in any way due to character; and if they are not, it is impossible that they should illustrate it.

It seems equally untrue that character can exist only as expressed in incident. We think of character generally as qualities which dispose people to a certain conduct; that is, as a capacity for a certain kind of action. Hence it is absurd to suppose that character cannot exist without action; if anything, it is rather the other way around. How can any action be characteristic if character does not have prior existence? It is quite possible that character is *best* expressed through incident, but certainly it may also be expressed in other ways, as any novel or drama can show.

Finally: is incident determined by character, and is it thus less important? That depends, I think, on what you mean. Certainly character determines action in *life*. Does it necessarily do so in fiction? There is no doubt that it does, when the incident is intended simply to illustrate character. By the same token, however, is there any doubt that it does not, when character is invented so that a given kind of incident may occur?

This leads us, of course, directly into the very old question of whether character is more important than plot. It is a question about which modern theorists have been extremely nervous; the ultimate decision has generally been in favor of character.

We may take as an instance the view of a great modern novelist. This is what E. M. Forster has to say:

"Character," says Aristotle, "gives us qualities, but it is in actions—what we do—that we are happy or the reverse." We have already decided that Aristotle was wrong, and now we must face the consequences of disagreeing with him. "All human happiness and misery," says Aristotle, "take the form of action." We know better. We believe that happiness and misery exist in the secret life, which each of us leads privately and to which (in his characters) the novelist has access. And by the secret life we mean the life for which there is no external evidence, not, as is vulgarly supposed, that which is revealed by a chance word or a sigh. A chance word or a sigh are just as much evidence as a speech or a murder: the life they reveal ceases to be secret and enters the realm of action.

This, if true, is very destructive to Aristotle's position that plot is the most important element in tragedy, since that position depends on the argument that "all human happiness and misery take the form of action." Forster does not actually conclude that plot is *less* important than character. He ends in a curious indecision: character can contribute too much or too little to plot, plot can demand too much of character, but we wind up in any case with a view "again unfavourable to Aristotle."

I am not going to try to refute Forster, although I have just apparently refuted Henry James. I say "apparently refuted" because I have not really done so: I have simply shown that his remarks are not without qualification true of all character and incident and of all relationships of these. Within their proper sphere, taken with reference to such literature as he had in mind, his observations are sound. It is very unlikely that a distinguished artist, thoughtful about his art, should be utterly mistaken about matters of his own experience; so unlikely, indeed, that if on a given point of art I had to choose between an absolute demonstration and the considered decision of the artist, I should feel compelled to accept the latter. I am not sure that art permits of absolute demonstration; I am positive that it entails experiences which are matters of fact and can be generalized.

The only difficulty with an artist's statements is that they are likely to be predicated upon a particular view, which we must take into consideration if we are to know *of what* the statements hold true. In the passages before us, for example, Forster seems to deny precisely what James seems to assert: that in the novel, character is realized only in external incident. Are we to take these writers as contradicting each other? Or shall we rather suppose that each had different aspects of the novel in view? The latter supposition appears not merely the more courteous but the more probable.

I assume thus, in this little contest between Forster

and Aristotle, that the question is not one of who is right and who is wrong, but one of in what sense, and in reference to what, each is asserting some kind of truth. Let us pass over Forster's interpretation of Aristotle; it is not as an interpreter of the *Poetics* but as an artist speaking of his art that he interests us. What he has in view is clearly this: that happiness and misery are inner feelings, and that consequently we ourselves alone know whether we are happy or wretched, and what makes us so; that the rest of the world can only conjecture our condition by our outward manifestations of it; and that it is the novelist only who has access through his art to the secret life of others, and who has that access only because he has invented them and made them what they are. He knows at the *source,* fully and completely, and independently of outward manifestations, for these are evident to anyone. Hence he ought to concern himself with that knowledge, primarily; and he ought not to permit the plot to make this a secondary matter. The plot consists of external actions, and, to the extent that he pays too much attention to it, he neglects the inner life.

I find this very plausible. But it is plausible only if we assume that the plot consists exclusively of external actions. Does it, in fact, in any serious work? Are not incidents in the soul as much incidents as fist-fights and horse-races? Is the "secret inner life" not activity? If not, what is it? It cannot consist in that case of thought or imagination or desires or emotions or even feelings of pleasure and pain; for all these come to be and pass away, are incidents in a process, are part of mental activity. And why must these be secret? Am I less happy or miserable simply because I give some outward token of my condition?

But surely the question should be clear by now. It is not a matter of plot at all. What Forster is really discussing is what we discussed in Chapter I: the difference between an action suited to narration and a dramatic action, as arising from a difference between what can be best recounted and what can best be acted out. And he seems to have come to the same conclusion that we did: that the dramatist is dependent upon external signs, whereas the novelist is not.

Well, you say, all very well. A happy ending. But which *is* the more important, plot or character?

And again I must say, that depends upon what you mean. If you mean by *most important* the most attractive element in a given form or a given work, the music may well be most important in certain forms of musical comedy, or character may be most important because you like a particular character better than anything else. I suppose it is this matter of attractiveness which led to the distinction between the novel of incident and the novel of character, against which Henry James protested so bitterly. Or if you mean *plot* in any of the senses which I dismissed somewhat earlier, I doubt very much whether it will turn out to be the most important element.

But if you mean *plot* in the sense in which I defined it, as a system of actions of a certain moral quality, there are a number of reasons for considering it more important than character.

We may assume, I think, that drama has an emotional effect upon us, whatever further effects it may have. Now, our emotions certainly have to do with the fortunes and misfortunes we witness; but these conditions come about through incident and action primarily, and through character only as it is conducive to action. Again, character functions in action; if it never eventuated in action, were never likely to, we should remain perfectly indifferent to it. Virtue and vice affect us emotionally because we recognize them as potentialities for certain kinds of action. We admire virtue and despise vice because of the kind of action to which they lead. Apart from such reflection on what they are likely to produce, they would have no significance for us. Moral qualities are like skills: the knowledge that a certain man is a great pianist may produce esteem but little else; but actually hearing him play is another matter; and there is such difference also between mere possession of a quality and the actual exercise of it. Again, character in drama, even when it changes in the course of the play, is relatively steadfast as compared with the rapid succession of incident on incident; the rapid alteration of our emotions shows that they must come from incident rather than character. The kinds and degrees of our emotions also show they they arise primarily from incident. We cannot pity a character without incident, we cannot hope for him without incident, we cannot fear him or fear for him apart from the expectation of incident. Finally, we often find that we undergo a whole process of emotions while character remains absolutely constant —something that would be impossible if character were the cause.

Beyond question, therefore, plot and incident are

primary. But, someone may object, what of "character drama"? What of "plot-less" drama, such as Chekhov's? And if plot is so important, why is not the "well-made" play the best of all possible plays?

These questions are easily answered. The unity and continuity even of character drama are effected by activity, not character; there are no character dramas in which the character remains merely in inert possession of his qualities. The "plot-less" drama is a mere chimera arising out of false analysis; anyone who thinks Chekhov's plays plot-less had better look at them again. The well-made play is rather an ill-made play, and it is ill-made primarily because of the impotence of its plot, in which all true power has been sacrificed to neatness of contrivance.

The argument whether plot or character is the more important is not intended to ascertain their relative social status, but to decide which shall govern which. We have decided that plot governs character. This is the reverse of the relation between character and action as these occur in life; in life it is generally character which governs action. I suppose the natural instance which is most closely parallel to what we are considering is that of finding someone who can occupy a given position or handle a particular job. When an executive has a position to fill, the job is the first consideration, and the man to hire is second. If a given kind of work is to be done properly, he must have a man qualified to do it. Similarly, if certain actions are to happen in the plot, and produce a given effect, a character must be invented or found who can perform them.

79

We are not, however, talking about what happens first in the creative process. Indeed, we are not talking about the creative process at all, but about the ultimate ordering which results from the creative process. A dramatist can begin with a number of characters and invent an action to suit them as Shaw claimed he did, or begin with an action and invent characters to suit it, as Dryden claimed he did, and the novelist can do the same thing. That is not the point at all; the point is that in the *finished* novel, or play, plot should properly govern. The *process* does not matter, except as it leads to the product; the *product* matters very much indeed. For my part, I am content to leave discussion of the creative process to the psychologists and others who write so knowingly about it; I am concerned with the product, and with the principles which make it what it is.

Another point: if the plot is to govern character, may it not turn that government into a tyranny? Or may not liberty become anarchy? Critics have often become more upset about these political metaphors than they have about the corresponding political facts. I do not know much about politics, but I know that in the good State the laws demand what the good Citizen does naturally and of his own volition. To escape from politics and put the question in Mr. Forster's terms: Can the plot demand too much or too little of the characters, can the characters contribute too much or too little to the plot, so that one or the other must suffer? Why, yes, of course that is possible. In fact, it is almost inevitable, when one or the other is badly conceived and contrived. It happens and happens, but it need not and should not happen. It will particularly tend to happen if you suppose that all plots must obey some such rule as "symmetry" or "complexity" or something of the kind; or if you feel that you must write a complete biography of every one of your characters whom you find at all interesting. It will also happen if you set up plot and character as extremes between which you will have to work out some reasonable compromise, on the mistaken notion that you are somehow then being fair and democratic. They are not extremes, and there is no compromise. In good construction they concur, and operate together.

We shall discover more about good construction in both as we proceed. In the meantime there are some points about character that ought to be considered as soon as possible. These can best be brought out, I believe, by considering what the fictitious character is, as opposed to a character in real life.

Let us take the real character first. I observe four different things about him. First, he was born with certain natural capacities. Second, as a consequence of education and the constant repetition of certain acts, he has formed habits and so has developed into a given kind of person, one of a certain moral character. Third, precisely because he is a certain kind of person, a certain bundle of habits, he will tend to act according to them. Fourth, he has a certain function or role in life; his profession or occupation in a very narrow sense, but more generally, some end which is his particular conception of what constitutes happiness.

Now look at a fictitious character. It would be absurd to say that he was born with certain natural capacities.

81

He is an artificial being. But it is unthinkable that he should be called upon to do things without being given the capacity to do them. Very well: let us give him some artificial capacities—ones *appropriate* to what he will have to do. Now, he has not really had education and has not really formed habits which make him into a certain kind of person. We may make him *like* a certain kind of person anyway, so that people will have certain opinions and feelings about him, just as if he were real. We can even invent a fictitious history if necessary, so that he may plausibly be what he is. But he still is not really what he seems to be; he has not really formed habits according to which he will tend to act. What can we do about that? Well, we can give him *consistency;* and if he is to act inconsistently, we will make him consistently inconsistent, just as habit would in real life. Finally, does he have a function in his artificial life? Indeed he has; in fact we invented him for just that. But we cannot allow him the freedom of a real person, then. He must act in a way *useful* to the plot. This last point is the whole foundation of his being, the reason for his being; and we gave him all he has, made him what he is, purely that he might be serviceable in this way.

There are four points, then, to be observed in the treatment of character: usefulness, appropriateness, likeness, and consistency. And now that I have said this, I remember that someone else said precisely the same thing.

The roles of characters will obviously differ in the different kinds of plot. It is quite conceivable, for example, that a consecutive plot should make different demands on character from those made by a descriptive plot, and the pattern plot or the didactic plot may make yet others. And the dramatic form makes a difference both in the functions and the kinds of characters: tragedy requires a different sort of protagonist from comedy, and farce, from melodrama. There are always, in addition, the exigencies of the particular work itself.

We saw earlier in this chapter that there were four general functions of incidents. Consequently there are four general functions of dramatic personages in reference to these. We have, thus, characters serving in essential, factorial, representational, or ornamental capacities. One and the same character may have different functions in different scenes of the same play; however, it is evident that sometimes a given character will serve in a single capacity throughout a whole play. Thus the protagonist is essential, since the essential action is impossible without him; certain characters involved only in factorial incidents are factorial; certain others who act merely as confidants or commentators, or who merely permit the continuity of representation, are representational; and those who exist merely for the sake of ornament are of course ornamental.

It must be apparent, too, that just as there is a matter of size or scale in incident—the incident merely as *conceived*, not represented—so there is also a matter of scale in character as conceived. Mr. Forster speaks of characters as "round" or "flat," and introduces another distinction, somewhat less formally, between the solid and the hollow. "Flat" characters are built around "a single idea or quality; when there is more than one

83

factor in them, we get the beginning of the curve toward the round." I am not sure what the difference between the "solid" and the "hollow" is. All I know about it is that "Pip and David Copperfield attempt roundness, but so diffidently that they seem more like bubbles than solids." Miss Elizabeth Bowen says, in her *Notes on Writing a Novel*, that Mr. Forster is quite wrong, that all characters should *ideally* be round, and presumably solid as well.

I am much too diffident to act as arbiter between Mr. Forster and Miss Bowen; consequently I will be bold enough to disagree with both of them. I observe that there are personages in both the novel and the drama who are not characterized at all, and who are consequently not even flat; and I observe that, from this minimal mere *presence,* scale ranges to characters of the highest degree of individuation. What is more, I do not want them, in many instances, to be anything more or less than they are, and should resent it bitterly if they were. I will simply say that a character should be adequate. Adequate to what? To his function, of course.

Characterization is much like drawing or painting. The artist may depict workers in a field as mere objects, men not really distinguishable from black tree-stumps. He may depict a very general human figure, so that we can say, "Someone is there," but not whether it is man or woman. He can go on and on in this fashion, growing more and more specific, until he reaches the absolute limit of individuation. The same range is possible in character, and I do not want to reduce that rich and various range to a matter of flat

and round. I want the character to do his job. If someone is raking leaves in the background while the hero
and the heroine are having their tragic conversation
in the autumn park, I am content that he should be
simply someone raking leaves. People do after all rake
leaves, and so long as he looks like someone raking
leaves, that is enough for me. I positively do not want
him "round"; in fact, I do not even want him "flat."
More than that: unless his raking those leaves adds
something somehow to what is going on, I want him
to quit raking them and just disappear. He should
never have existed in the first place. Someone has
praised Colette for asking a young writer, "What kind
of trees were they, that you said were barely visible in
the far distance?" I will not praise her for that: I think
it is a silly question.

But what about making characters vivid? And moving? And convincing?

We have already talked about making them convincing. Make them useful, give them appropriate capacities, make them resemble certain kinds of persons,
make them consistent; that is to make them convincing.
As for vividness, that is a matter of representation;
and that we must take up next. Before we move on to
that, we must mention a somewhat tired old distinction between stable and dynamic characters—between,
that is, characters who do not change in the course
of the plot and characters who do. There is nothing
here that has not already been covered in the fore-
going.

IV
The Elements of Drama: Representation and Dialog

SO FAR we have been talking only about dramatic ideas. Plot, incident, character—these are all conceptions; even the dramatist who has worked these out as fully as possible would not have had occasion to write a single word, except by way of notes. And he does not yet have a *play* in any sense. He has not yet determined what actions are to be shown upon the stage. Where does the play begin? Or end? What, if anything, is to happen offstage? What happens in what order onstage? How long or short, in terms of acting-time, is a given scene to be?

It is impossible to enact a play unless these and similar questions have been answered. On the other hand, the moment they have been answered—no matter how crudely and generally—acting does become possible, a play of a sort has come into existence. The *representation* or scenario has been devised. The difference between the crudest and most general scenario and the most detailed script, complete with full stage directions and dialog in which every inflection has been indicated, is not that one is a play and the other is not, but that more or less is left to the director's or the actor's decision, that more or less is under the playwright's control. Drama is comparable to music in this respect. An ancient composer often indicated a place for a cadenza or an embellishment without further specification, or indicated the harmony and left the figuration to the performer. Modern composers tend to determine performance in minute detail. But both compose music, as soon as some sort of performance is indicated. So with drama.

The *commedia dell'arte,* according to tradition, operated on the barest outlines, which the actors filled out with improvisation or with stock business and set speeches. Some doubts have been raised recently as to whether this happened in fact or not; but whether fact or not, the practice is perfectly possible, and that is all that need concern us. Indeed, it is more than possible, whatever the practice of the *commedia dell'arte.* Dramatic literature contains many perfectly general directions such as "Here Erode ragis in the pagond and in the strete also" in *The Magi, Herod, and the Slaughter of the Innocents,* or Tom Robertson's "Enter Waiter . . . and receives orders" in *Society.*

We find, thus, further confirmation of our view that drama is not essentially a form of literature, but rather a distinct art which may or may not employ language as an artistic medium. It is literary only through its employment of dialog, though Shaw, for one, has made it literary through its stage directions and through dramatic prefaces as well; and while, beyond all doubt, the highest forms of drama demand dialog, dialog itself cannot be regarded as the most important element, though it is frequently thought of as precisely that. On the contrary, it is a subsidiary part. Without it, certainly, a great number of subtle effects would be impossible; more than that, the profundity of great drama would be impossible; but these very considerations show that it is simply the medium through which these effects are achieved, under the governance of plot. The dialog exists to give the plot its quality and power; therefore it is subordinate to plot. Since the representation determines when dialog is proper and when it is not, and what the nature of dialog shall be, the dialog is also subordinate to the representation. Indeed, in one aspect, the dialog is simply an extension of the representation, detailing what words shall be said in what order.

The representation obviously functions as a plan for acting and speaking, so far as the performers are concerned. And it functions, so far as the playwright is concerned, as the instrument of his control over the performers. Both of these functions, however, have their foundation in one which is more important still: the production of the proper effect upon the audience. The playwright controls the performance so that he may ultimately control the response of the audience.

How does the representation permit that ultimate control? By determining what the audience is to know at a given time, and so determining what they are to feel. We must leave the full investigation of the audience's reactions to the next chapter; for the present, we need only observe that a relation between knowledge and emotion exists, and that both are produced by the representation. Once the curtain has risen, what is said and done upon the stage soon informs us about the persons of the drama, their moral character and their situation, and what good or bad fortune may be anticipated for them. We need hardly argue that our emotional responses are based upon such information.

More particularly, the representation determines what shall be given our principal attention, the vividness with which we shall realize it, the length of time we shall be concerned with it, the context of recollection and anticipation in which we shall take it, what inferences we are to draw from it, the general light in which we shall regard it. On the whole, however, two general principles underlie the representation, and these, as we shall see, resolve to a single one. These are principles of probability and of emotional effect.

They constitute, that is, the most general answers to the question *why* a particular scene should or should not be enacted upon the stage. Why must we see Antony in the very act of convincing the Roman rabble? Certainly it is an effective scene; even more, it is required by probability. The event is not *generally probable;* but under particular circumstances it is probable, and we must see it as occurring under those circumstances, especially since the whole later part of the action depends upon it. Why, in *Antony and Cleopatra,* is it better to have Enobarbus describe Cleopatra upon her barge than to display the scene itself upon the stage? Because the scene itself could produce only a general impression of luxury and splendor; whereas we must feel the power of Cleopatra's enchantment as affecting even an enemy, so that we accept her subsequent power over Antony. Why is it a dramatic fault, in *As You Like It*, to give the conversion of Oliver and of the Duke in narrative, rather than to show it upon the stage? Because it is not generally probable that two men who feel deep-seated and unnatural hatred for their brothers should suddenly change their attitudes. The whole complication here rests upon that hatred; the resolution is to be produced by removal of that hatred; and the narrative even of the special circumstances that produced the change cannot impress us as forcibly as enacted action. Consequently the resolution seems implausible and arbitrary.

To make a quick induction, then: a scene should be represented even though it is not part of the plot, if its representation strengthens the probability or the effect of the action; and conversely, even though it is part of the plot, it should not be represented if it weakens the probability or the effect of the action. As we remarked much earlier, some things that are probable as described cease to be so when set before our eyes, and some things that produce one effect when described produce a contrary one when enacted. If you wrote a tragedy on the subject of Thyestes, you would do very wrong, I think, to show on stage the killing, butchering, cleaning, seasoning, and cooking of the children who are served to their father. Pity and fear would instantly cease, and be supplanted by violent revulsion. The event is utterly revolting even in description, as you may quickly discover by looking it up in Seneca's *Thyestes,* where it is given in tasteless and senseless detail.

Events of general probability, all other things being equal, can be omitted from the representation. If you call the police, they usually come; if they apprehend the criminal, he is usually convicted and punished; hence many a curtain drops, in mystery plays, with the summoning of the police; the rest can be taken for granted, and can add nothing. Here a whole train of consequences is cut short, because it is all present by implication. In a similar way, a whole train of antecedent events, even within the action, can be omitted, because they are present by implication in some event which is their effect, and which could only have been produced by them. Thus you need not be shown, step by step, the growth of remorse in Lady Macbeth, or the progression which leads to her illness and somnambulism. The whole is made clear by the sleepwalking scene itself.

We may apply these principles to the matter of beginning as well. Where the initial situation is a highly complex one, where we must have fairly well established attitudes toward the characters if we are to feel the full effect, where the initiating incident of the plot is probable or effective only with some preparation, the representation must begin before the beginning of the plot itself. In any opposite case, the representation may begin simultaneously with the plot, or even somewhat after. It is a question of how much we need to know, and what we have to feel, in advance. *Hamlet* and *Othello* require representations beginning well before the plot does; *King Lear* can have the plot begin almost simultaneously with the representation.

It is well known that certain events are far more powerful when left to the imagination than when set before us. The principle behind this is, I believe, a simple one: that when a deed—let us say, a horrific one—is left indeterminate, the mind imagines it as happening in a number of different ways, all of them horrific, and reacts to the compounded horror of all of them; whereas the representation can show the event as determinate only, as happening in only one of the possible ways. Scenes are also omitted, of course, for purposes of suspense and surprise merely.

Not all of the represented scenes function to give probability or emotional power to the plot. Some have their function in the representation itself. They permit continuity, facilitate exits and entrances, retain a character on scene for some reason, or simply afford the occasion for some ornament. The famous Porter's scene in *Macbeth* is of this order, although it is so magnificently handled that its basic function has seldom been recognized. In the scene preceding, Macbeth has become bemused and paralyzed with horror at his deed. In this situation he is incapable of action: Lady Macbeth must go herself to restore the daggers and incriminate the grooms. A lesser dramatist would have ended the scene with her returning and leading Macbeth off to bed; Shakespeare invents the appalling termination that we all know. Abrupt and unforeseen intervention; a knocking which can arouse the whole household; detection threatened precisely at the point where the murderer can stir neither hand nor foot to prevent it. Marvelous: but a problem comes with it. Once there is such a knocking, who is to answer the door? Unless we see the answering of the door, we shall have a break in the action. A break in the action is unthinkable; so we have a scene to keep the continuity, but such a scene as handled by Shakespeare.

When the plot is polylinear, there are several possibilities of representation. The main line may be represented, but none of the sub-lines, as in *Oedipus Tyrannus;* or the main line may be represented with all or some of the sub-lines, as in *King Lear;* or the sub-lines may be shown while the main action takes place off-stage, as in *The Sea-Gull.* A line can be shown completely or incompletely; for example, the Laertes line in *Hamlet* can be said to be shown in full, even though we do not see what Laertes did in Paris; his going away and coming back are all that is relevant to the plot. The Fortinbras line, on the other hand, is incompletely shown: we merely get glimpses of him at different stages in his fortunes. The same principles apply to sub-lines which operate in main lines; that is, the incidents in a sub-line should be shown on stage as probability or effect or continuity require. Whether the sub-line should be represented at all or given dominant representation depends, of course, upon the main line. We have seen that sub-lines can mirror the main line, or be in sharp contrast to it, or offer both resemblances and differences. The powerful effects which can be produced by such reflection or contrast are familiar to everyone. In general they serve the intellectual purpose of focussing the attention of the audience upon elements of the action that might otherwise have gone unnoticed, and they serve the emotional purpose of bringing out more sharply the effective factors in the action. In *Hamlet,* for instance, Fortinbras shows us what a prince in Hamlet's situation might have done, and Laertes shows us what the son of a murdered father might have done. Both emphasize things that Hamlet himself does or does not do. This is a matter of emphasis. In *Anna Karenina,* the happiness of Dolly and Levin makes us feel more keenly the misery of Anna. This is a matter of emotional enhancement.

Some actions, of their very nature, seem to call for other lines of action than the main one. For example, some plots have their whole significance in the similar or different reactions of different people in a given situation. Plays like Philip Barry's *Hotel Universe* or Sir James M. Barrie's *Dear Brutus* would dissolve into nothing, so to speak, without multiple lines. Again, a play like Goldoni's *The Servant of Two Masters* would be utterly impossible as a single line, for the whole action and its effect depend precisely upon the servant's difficulties in playing the double role. Other actions, of their very nature, have their conclusion clearly foreseeable from their initiating actions, or from their early complication. If the hero can only decline further and further in his fortunes, or if he can only continue to prosper, the audience becomes bored and indifferent; consequently a sub-line must be invented to make the outcome less certain. Otherwise neither surprise nor suspense is possible; and, what is more important, the emotional effect must decrease even though the fortunes of the protagonist become markedly better or worse. Marlowe's *Doctor Faustus* (a terribly poor play, whatever the poets say!) is an instance of real mis-handling of this sort. A sub-line should have been invented to make the catastrophe less inevitable; indeed, the main line itself should have avoided such puerile horseplay as Faustus engages in; it should have concentrated upon the anguish of a man who sells his soul.

When the main line itself is very short, and nevertheless is to be extended to a length suitable for a full-sized play, a "stretcher" of some sort is required. There are many "stretching" devices; the invention of complicating sub-lines is the best, whether a built-in or initial complication is used or whether the complication is merely incidental. The usefulness of a sub-line which does not complicate is dependent upon the particular case. In *Doctor Faustus*—since we have mentioned that—the underplot does not complicate the main line and clearly weakens the whole play, even though Wagner and his adventures constitute a kind of comic mirror of the actions of Faustus himself.

In all instances in which a sub-line is required, there is the possibility that it must also be represented. Again the dramatist must solve this problem by considering whether such representation makes for greater probability or emotional power. It must not be supposed that the more powerful is always necessarily the more desirable. The important thing is that the play should have its proper emotional quality. The sub-line may be so powerful as to overshadow the main line, or so uneventful as to be dull. In such cases it should never be represented. Its power may be modified, if it is represented, by showing only its convergence with or its divergence from the main line, where, to use my earlier phrase, these "threaten"; or by showing only the crucial developments of the subline, or the crux itself, or the after-effects. The main line itself, when it is to be the object of contemplation rather than of intense emotion, should go unrepresented, at least in its more emotional parts; perhaps even as a whole. We cannot contemplate events or see them accurately when we are intensely excited or when we are swept rapidly from emotion to emotion; and contemplation can, in the end, be more deeply moving than unreflecting excitement. The events of the main action may be of a sort which naturally lends itself to melodramatic treatment, and yet the intention of the dramatist may have nothing to do with the sensationalism of melodrama. Some of E. M. Forster's novels illustrate very well what I mean. Their plots contain death-scenes, scenes of suffering and violence, and so on, which would have induced Dickens to use all his eloquence and invention to bring out their fullest effect; yet Forster barely touches on them, even passes over them, as in no way his main concern. As I have already remarked, Chekhov does something very similar in leaving melodramatic incidents off-stage, even when they are in the main line of action. The famous Chekhovian pistol-shots are, for the dramatist as for us, a secondary matter; the interesting thing is what led up to them.

Anything that is represented is by that very fact given immediacy, imminency, closeness; indeed, the

97

principle behind "arena theatre" and "audience participation" is one of making that imminency or closeness even greater. And anything represented is given definiteness and certainty; we see it as it is. By the same token, anything not represented is made remote and indefinite. It must be remote at least in the sense of being somewhat distant from us or concealed from us; since it *is* concealed, it can only be as definite as our own inference or someone's report may allow. Now, not merely the *degree* but even the *kind* of our emotion depends upon the imminence of the event and our own involvement in it, or the closeness of our relation to those involved, as well as upon our certainty or uncertainty. What may cause intense grief when it is imminent in time or place may cause a gentle melancholy when it is remote. What evokes pity for those who are not close to us may cause terror when it threatens those who are close. Hope and fear can exist only where there is some uncertainty; certainty turns them to joy or grief. Obviously the dramatist must take all such matters into consideration.

We have already seen that an incident, to be probable and effective, must be of a certain scale as a *conceived* incident; it must also be of a certain scale in its representation. In the first place, it cannot be of so brief a duration that it passes unnoticed, for then it might as well never have been represented at all; nor can it be protracted to the point where it fails to hold the attention. What is more, in any drama which is realistic in its depiction—that is, any which employs natural signs and the real or apparent doing of the imitated actions—the acting must correspond in both

length of time and *tempo* to the length and *tempo* of
the imitated action. Otherwise the actions will be too
rapid or too slow, will be accomplished in too brief or
too long a time, and will appear ridiculous. Watch an
old-fashioned movie, and you will see what I mean;
the characters appear, in modern projection, to scurry
about in ludicrous fashion. A slow-motion movie will
give you the other half of the matter. The acting-time
of the play itself need not correspond to the time
supposedly covered by the plot; that is another affair
entirely. But certain processes and actions necessarily
require a certain amount of time. A portrait, for instance, cannot be executed in a moment; on the other
hand, it is usually absurd and pointless to represent
such processes of execution at length. It is far better
to show only a phase or two, and to make these phases
imply whatever is relevant or effective in the process
itself.

For example, Lady Macbeth's illness—if it is that—
is a long-drawn-out process. It would be ineffective to
show the whole even if time allowed; Shakespeare
solves the problem by a single very brief scene which
sets before us all the shocking ravages of her remorse.
Strictly speaking, the scene is one of representation
purely, for neither the Doctor nor the Gentlewoman
acts in consequence of their knowledge; the scene exists simply to show her dreadful condition.

The nature of the action or process is not, however,
the only determinant here. Character and circumstance also operate to determine the length and the
speed of an action. A deliberate man will have to do
whatever he does deliberately, and a quick man,

99

quickly. Murder of one man will be an easy matter, murder of another difficult. Similarly, what can be done rapidly under certain circumstances may take a good deal of time under others. All of these factors must be considered.

Besides, the scene must have its own proper emphasis. It must offer adequately all the emotional factors requisite to its effect, and in such a fashion that the more important stand out more clearly than the less important; and of course it should have no more or less emphasis, as a scene, than is proper to its place in the whole. A minor scene should not occupy a great deal of time, in the acting, while a major one flashes by in a moment. But all of these problems, I think, can be settled by considering the function of the scene together with the elements which make it probable and effective.

Certain properties of representation in drama become clear when we compare it with its parallel in narrative, the narrative device. Everyone knows that a novel may be told in the first or the third person; that the narrator may be someone outside the action or within it; that the narration may be in the form of letters or memoirs or a diary or a history.

The choice of a narrative device is by no means arbitrary. It makes a great deal of difference *how* the novel is told. If *Don Quixote* were narrated by the Don himself, it would turn into one more chivalric romance. If it were told by Sancho Panza, the chivalric element might be totally lost. If it were told by some other person within the novel, that person would have to accompany the Knight and his Squire on their ad-

ventures; and if he had sufficient intelligence to understand what was happening, as he must to narrate it
properly, he would in all likelihood have prevented
the adventures. The narrator must consequently be
someone outside the action. If we pushed this analysis
further, we should find that he had to have other
characteristics as well. To take another instance: the
whole effect of *Jonathan Wild* depends upon having
a narrator who treats everything ironically, so that
the villain appears as an exemplar of "greatness,"
while the virtuous characters appear as "low,"
"mean," or "foolish." One more example: in *Barry
Lyndon* the first-person narrator engages our sympathy until we begin to disapprove of his picaresque adventures, and ultimately we are glad to learn that he
is in prison, where he certainly belongs.

Is there a similar relation between the dramatic
plot and its representation? There is. A play can have
a "narrator," like the Chorus in *Doctor Faustus* or
Tom in *The Glass Menagerie*. It can offer part of itself as "Reality" and part as "Fiction": thus in *Fanny's
First Play* and Sheridan's *The Critic*—in both of
which we have a play within a play—we are to take
the inner play as a play, but the outer one as reality.
Or this can be reversed: thus the inner play in *Six
Characters in Search of an Author* is a supposed in-
trusion of reality into the illusory world of the play
which the actors are trying to rehearse. There are
plays which produce their effects by pretending tem-
porarily that they are "real"; and there are plays
which produce their effects by insisting that they are
plays and nothing but plays, and by doing any num-

101

ber of things to shatter the "dramatic illusion." It would be a long story to go into all of these devices of representation; it is sufficient, doubtless, to point out that they exist, that they must be reckoned with, that there should be a reason for adopting one rather than another of them, and that, once you have begun to use one of them, you must have a good reason to abandon it. A dramatic device carries probabilities of its own and sets up its own probabilities which must be resolved. A case in point is *The Taming of the Shrew:* once Shakespeare chose to set the main play within the framework of the Christopher Sly episodes, he ought to have carried out the plan. I suppose everyone who knows the play feels some disappointment that the Sly story was abandoned, with only one further reference, and that we shall never know how it concluded.

A given representative device has certain distinctive technical advantages and disadvantages. For example, if you use a "narrator" like the Stage Manager in *Our Town,* you do away at once with all the problems of producing motivated exits and entrances, for the Stage Manager need simply summon and dismiss the characters, and problems of continuity in general are reduced to a minimum. On the other hand, the very arbitrariness of the Stage Manager's behavior makes definite anticipation impossible, and so obviates the possibility of any very powerful suspense or surprise. The device works beautifully in its own play; it would be disastrous in others.

A bold overall device of this kind, shrewdly employed, will impress an audience greatly; but I believe that the very greatest drama has never used anything of this sort. Shakespeare, for example, never uses the representative devices which appeal to Pirandello and Wilder; he is content with simply arranging the representation so that scene by scene we take the view he wishes us to take. Consider, for example, the murder of Duncan. It is a dastardly, an unnatural, a monstrous act. Were we to see Macbeth commit it, it would leave us with an indelible impression of brutality which would preclude all sympathy for him. It must remain a hideous murder; but it must happen off stage; and we must see the indecision, the revulsion, the agitation and anguish of the murderer before the crime, and the remorse, horror, and fear which follow immediately upon it. This is in fact what we do see; and Shakespeare forces us to be more concerned for the murderer than for his victim. The proof of this is that at the knocking—closely as it follows upon the murder—we are actually fearful for Macbeth. The suffering which takes place before our eyes is so immediate and so intense that the murder of Duncan, base as it is, is comparatively remote and faint. In the sleepwalking scene—to take another instance—we are led gradually but swiftly to accept the incredible breakdown of Lady Macbeth; Shakespeare makes us see it from the point of view of the skeptical and calm Doctor. We become convinced with him, and ultimately share his wondering horror at what he sees.

Representation ranges from the bluntness of direct statement to the refinement of extremest subtlety. In Plautus' *Menaechmi* Peniculus enters, identifies himself, describes his own character, states his relation to

Menaechmus, identifies Menaechmus' house (as well as Menaechmus himself presently), and declares his present business, all in direct statement to the audience. A somewhat more sophisticated dramaturgy would bring all this out in conversation—one of the commonest forms is a conversation between two servants—in a scene especially constructed for exposition and having no particular interest beyond that of the information conveyed. A subtler art, still using such a scene, substitutes implication for direct statement. A subtler still goes farther and gives such scenes a powerful interest in their own right. The mature Shakespeare makes his exposition into a story of high interest in its own right, as in the first Act of *Othello*, or casts it into powerful episodes, as in *Hamlet*.

The more representation depends upon implication, the greater tends to be its dependence upon signs. We have already said a good deal about signs, but there are some further aspects of them that we must look into. We can distinguish signs, first of all, according to how much they imply. A complete sign is one single thing which indicates a single thing, such as a trait, an emotion, a physical condition, the probability of an act, and so on. An incomplete sign is one which requires conjunction with other signs to complete its implication. A multiple sign is one which, itself single, permits a number of inferences, either all at once or successively. For example, from one remark we may infer at once a whole group of traits, perhaps even the whole character; or our inferences may be successive, as when the remark leads us to infer an emotion from which we infer a desire from which we infer character from which in turn we infer a probability of action.

Thus Brabantio's "How! The Duke in Council!" is a complete sign, simply implying surprise. Roderigo's first speech, "I take it much unkindly . . . that thou shouldst know of this," tells us nothing beyond what it directly says; we must know more to see what it implies. This is an incomplete sign. Othello's "Keep up your bright swords, for the dew will rust them," is a multiple sign. We can infer from it all the better part of his character. He says this immediately after Brabantio has insulted him. In saying this, he ignores the insult. We infer at once that he is not easily stirred to anger, for the insult is extreme, and that he is perfectly assured of the justice of his case. A small-minded man would have resented the imputation; Othello shows himself generous of mind. The insult is incidental to Brabantio's command to attack him— "Down with him, thief!"—and in fact Othello's situation is one of some danger; he ignores the danger, too, and shows himself brave. But his bravery is not the posturing sort that we find in the romantic hero; it is the bravery of a man to whom danger is so familiar and courage so habitual that he is perfectly at ease. It is not the courage merely of a sanguine temperament, or of anger, or of ignorance; it has finer sources than these.

Othello is so much at ease that he can joke, and joke about the very point of danger, the swords, and do it in the relaxed and dignified way of gentle irony. No sarcasm; no contempt; only mildness. His one concern, he implies, is for the enemies who threaten him, or rather for the weapons with which they threaten him. The weapons may be damaged; not in combat, of course, but by exposure to the dews; that is the only danger. Shouts, torches, glittering swords, an angry mob; and amid all this tumult the calm, motionless Othello, displaying in a speech of eleven words all the qualities which set him apart from the rest. Who else is thinking at this moment of the *night,* the *dews,* the *brightness* of the swords rather than of their keenness? The crisis of Act I is not over by any means, but events have taken a different turn, and Othello has made them do so in one brief speech. So much may be implicit in one action.

Signs may be emotionally affecting in themselves, as well as in their reference. For example, the fact that a lamp has not been turned on in a room may indicate that someone is too despondent to do so; we are moved when we infer the despondency, but it is that which moves us, and not the lamp itself. On the other hand, we are affected by tears or moans in themselves, as well as by what they indicate. The immediate effect always sets its cause more vividly before us than one requiring a chain of inferences, and the immediate cause suggests its effect more vividly than a remote one. We are so constituted that the pain or pleasure of others, even animals, is not indifferent to us, and we respond to any indication of such pain or pleasure with great sensitivity on the whole. We respond according to the nature, the degree, and what I shall call the importance of the pain or pleasure; consequently we are moved more definitely in general by *special* than we are by *common* signs: by signs, that is, which tend to give us special information about the condition. For example, many emotions involve agitation; we respond to someone's agitation with a certain general uneasiness, but we do not react with very definite emotions until we have more definite indications as to his condition.

I believe that it is the almost constant use of common signs which accounts for the general flatness of the heroic drama of the Neo-Classical period in England. The heroes and heroines of such drama are very often mere bundles of general traits and emotions—the abstract virtues in high degree, the abstract noble passions and emotions—which seem a matter of definition, of hypothesis, even, rather than a matter of human nature and its history. Once they are assumed, every action and passion is pretty clearly foreseeable, as a deduction from the definition. I do not think that there is such ease of prediction in the behavior of fully realized characters. One can easily tell what Dryden's Antony or his Cleopatra would do in a given situation; can one say the same of Shakespeare's? I cannot imagine that Dryden's Antony would tease Cleopatra as she helped him with his armor, or that Dryden's Cleopatra would "hop forty paces through the public street," or be breathless if she did. They are not alive enough for that. If we are really to depict human beings, our depictions must have both a certain definiteness and, underlying that, a certain mystery. For that is how human beings are—we may know them intimately, and yet they are mysterious.

One notices a certain difficulty that both dramatists and novelists have in depicting characters of a given profession or occupation. I have always doubted that

107

Oswald Alving could really paint, that Halvard Solness could really build, that Dryden's Antony could command an army, and that most of Henry James's writers could write. On the other hand, I have never doubted that Hamlet was a prince and a scholar, that Macbeth, Othello, and Coriolanus were generals, that Lear was a king.

How does this conviction or lack of conviction come about? Hollywood, whenever it wants to convince us that someone is a painter or a pianist, will always show him painting or playing. Personally, I am never convinced by any of that. Is it mere prejudice on my part, like that of the audiences of Dryden's time, who—according to his Lisideius—laughed at death-scenes because they knew that the actor was not really dying? Possibly it is; but I doubt it. I think it is a matter of common signs, drawn from too easy and simple-minded a conception of what a poet or painter or pianist is like. We are all very largely products of our own individual history, which leaves its marks upon us; our occupation or profession, as a fairly permanent part of that history, leaves very definite marks, which show up in almost everything we do. We are also people of one sort or another by nature; and the marks of one and the same profession show up quite differently in different sorts of people. I believe, thus, that in handling his major characters, the writer does better to show us these distinctive marks—*special signs*—rather than common ones. Otherwise he may be far wiser simply to inform us that So and So is a thus and thus, and let it go at that. In other words, the writer ought to give us the sense that the character he has invented has been *caused, formed:* not simply assumed.

Signs obviously are more efficient—*do* more—when they are distinctive, for they then imply a great many more general things under which they fall, whereas common signs are so general in themselves that there is little left of greater generality for them to imply. It is much like the matter of predications: if I say "Englishman," I imply *man, animal, living being, existence,* but if I say "animal," I imply only *living being* and *existence.* The same thing applies to what is implied: a sign which indicates a given emotion merely cannot be distinctive. We are all liable to emotions, and no one is of this or that disposition simply because of this. To exhibit fear before what anyone and everyone would regard as fearful, thus, is not "characteristic" (though *not* to exhibit it would be!); but to exhibit such and such a kind and degree of emotion, in a certain frame of mind, at a certain object, and so on—this is a definite indication of character.

Signs can be ambiguous or clear, and this is a different matter from being common or special, or any of the other things we have been considering. A sign is clear if it is exactly what it seems to be and implies exactly what we think it implies; otherwise it is ambiguous. Suppose we see a man running out of a house where a murder has been committed. The mere fact of his running is an ambiguous sign. If we interpret his running as *running away,* we infer that he is either guilty or liable to suspicion; if we interpret it as *running in pursuit* of a criminal, we infer his innocence. Here we have a sign ambiguous in itself. But he may in fact have been *running away,* and yet for another reason than guilt or fear of suspicion; and this is ambiguity, not of the sign, but of its reference. In brief: there is a difference between uncertainty as to what a given sign is, and uncertainty as to what it signifies.

Incomplete signs are frequently ambiguous when they seem to be complete, so that we draw the inference, only to be supplied later with an additional factor that changes the whole picture. Do not suppose that such devices are useful only for mystery stories. On the contrary, they lie at the root of some of the profoundest and subtlest revelations of character that we have. *King Lear,* as we shall see, depends heavily upon the ambiguous sign, and the failure to recognize this has led to reams of critical nonsense.

A sign, to have its effect, must be evident to the audience. How can they infer anything from something they do not observe? Here one might think to find a difficulty, for not every actor can blush or grow pale, and perhaps it would not be visible to the audience in any case. In fact, however, the problem can be solved by dialog: one actor can comment on what would be invisible in the expression or conduct of another, or what would otherwise escape attention. The crudest method is the comment which does nothing but bring out the sign, as in Stephen Phillips' "Ulysses lives— thou art gone white." The subtlest method is the Shakespearian device, in which the sign itself produces a particularly dramatic effect upon the character who observes it—an effect usually of great significance:

MACB.: The devil damn thee black, thou cream-
faced loon!
Where got'st thou that goose look?
SERV.: There is ten thousand—
MACB.:   Geese, villain?
SERV.:   Soldiers, sir.
MACB.: Go prick thy face and over-red thy fear,
Thou lily-livered boy. What soldiers,
patch?
Death of thy soul! Those linen cheeks of
thine
Are counsellors to fear. What soldiers,
whey-face?
SERV.: The English force, so please you.
MACB.: Take thy face hence.

All signs are devices, and have their special uses;
they are best particularly, therefore, when they best
suit their particular function. A multiple sign can be
a mistake if it allows the audience to know too much
at a given point; an ambiguous sign can be excellent
if it is intended to lead the audience to a false inference, so that they can be surprised later; an incomplete
sign can produce extraordinary suspense. But in general we may say that a given sign is best when it is one
which a character would naturally have exhibited,
and when it arises in the very course of action and sets
the bloom of life upon *it*. All this is a very important
part of what we mean when we say that character and
action are vivid and convincing; and why I say this
should be obvious enough by now.

I remember that I have another topic in this chapter—the topic of dialog—about which I have said very

little. At least it may seem so. In my own view, I have practically covered it. The dialog has a special function in the representation. It offers us many signs, and so sets action and character before us, vividly and convincingly. Besides that, if it is long, it makes the scene long, so it is clearly related to the important business of representative scale. It makes possible the representation of many things—complicated thought, delicate shades of passion, for example, that would not otherwise be possible.

Can we say more about it?

Well, we can; but I think that in the present state of dramatic affairs we might lean in the direction of saying only a little more. Beyond question a stilted, a trite, a bombastic, a feeble, or simply dull dialog can ruin a play. It does so, however, primarily because it fails, as dialog, to be vividly appropriate to the characters, because it fails as a presentation of *signs*.

Let us take as an instance Sir Walter Scott, who could not write dialog. I will cast a more or less exciting episode in *The Talisman* into dramatic form, simply by excerpting the speeches as he wrote them:

KING RICHARD: We must be near the station, and yonder cavalier is one of Saladin's outposts—methinks I hear the noise of the Moorish horns and cymbals. Get into order, my hearts, and form yourselves around the ladies soldierlike and firmly.

DE VAUX: Were it not well, my liege, to send a page to the top of that sandbank? Or would it stand with your pleasure that I prick forward? Methinks, by all yonder clash and clang, if there be no more than five hundred men beyond the sand-hills, half of the Soldan's men must be drummers and cymbal-tossers.—Shall I spur on?

KING RICHARD: Not for the world. Such a caution would express suspicion, and could do little to prevent surprise, which, however, I apprehend not.

That is not very good, certainly. What is wrong with it?

Something very simple, I should say. It does not sound in the least like people talking in an exciting situation. In fact, it does not sound like people talking. I do not find any particular indication of character or emotion; so far as I am concerned, I had just as soon have it in indirect discourse, in somebody else's words. That is really what it is, anyway; Sir Walter Scott's words. He has not asked himself who and what his characters really are, what they feel, or particularly what they think; he has not tried to stand in their shoes, feel what they feel, and say what they would say as they would say it. In short, this is dead as a door-nail because the author has never made the people live. There are no *signs* of life.

But is that all we can say? What about beautiful language? What about beautiful verse?

Suppose we look at what Granville-Barker called "magical speech."

MACB.:   Wherefore was that cry?
SEYTON: The queen, my lord, is dead.

113

MACB.:   She should have died hereafter;
           There would have been a time for such
             a word.
           To-morrow, and to-morrow, and to-
             morrow
           Creeps in this petty pace from day to day
           To the last syllable of recorded time,
           And all our yesterdays have lighted fools
           The way to dusty death. Out, out, brief
             candle!
           Life's but a walking shadow, a poor
             player
           That struts and frets his hour upon the
             stage
           And then is heard no more; it is a tale
           Told by an idiot, full of sound and fury,
           Signifying nothing.

This is certainly very beautiful—magical in the sense of having an enchanting effect upon us, which is what Granville-Barker meant. But if "magical" is taken to mean that we cannot discover why it is beautiful, or that, as E. K. Chambers puts it, "an exact analysis of these lines is impossible"—why, this I deny absolutely.

This is a speech, let us remember, in a play; it is not a lyric, and consequently cannot exhibit the organization of a self-contained whole. In a lyric, character and situation are always far more general than they can be in a play; and, because there is no larger context of action in which we can place the lyric, no larger frame of reference in which we can consider it, we can have only a momentary, at least a very brief, acquaintance with the person exhibited in it. He comes to us without any history; we can only know very generally, if at all, what he has done and felt before; and once his moment of thought or passion is over, he disappears without a trace. The lyric poet can only display such action, thought, character, and passion as can be made intelligible and effective on the basis of such short acquaintance. No matter how profound the thought or subtle the passion, no matter how cryptic the expression of it, all that is needed to understand the human activity depicted must lie within the brief span of the lyric speech itself.

The speeches in drama are so entirely different from this that a play made up of lyrics—a play in which each speech was an independent lyric—would be intolerable. Indeed, it is not done even in lyric drama. And a dramatic speech is likely to be "impossible to analyze" if you try to treat it as a lyric poem.

We must recall, if we are to see the meaning and the force of this speech, something of the play itself. We must recall that Macbeth is a man who, at the beginning of the play, has everything that he might be supposed to desire. He is a military hero who has just won a desperate and crucial war. He is beloved and admired by all. He is first in the King's favor and first among all the nobles. He is of the royal line. He has wealth, strength, a devoted wife, and excellent promise (leaving the Witches quite aside) of even better fortune to follow. And it is not enough. He is so close to supreme power in Scotland that a single deed can give it to him. But even kingship is not enough: he must secure it forever for his heirs. At the incitation of his wife he does what he must do to obtain the throne; gains it, to find kingship meaningless, to forfeit his peace of mind (and his hope of heaven), to live in an ever-worsening nightmare of fear and bloodshed, and eventually to lose all he has, even hope itself. He has thrown away a rich present for a dream of the future; he has gambled for hope and won fear.

He speaks the speech we are considering when he senses that catastrophe is imminent. The Scotch revolt which was only a "rumour" in Act IV has become revolution; Macbeth has gone into the field against it, only to be driven back and forced to shut himself up in Dunsinane castle. Presently there is news of Malcolm's invasion; presently, news that the royal thanes, Menteith, Caithness, Lennox, and Angus, with all their clans, have gone over to Malcolm's side; presently, news that an English force of ten thousand is at hand. His castle is then besieged; as his foes pour at him, innumerable, and at the very walls, as he is in the act of issuing commands, intent upon the danger without and heartening himself and his men against it, he hears a terrible cry from *within*. He *says* at this point that he has "almost forgot the taste of fears" and that "direness cannot once start" him, and commentators have rashly believed him, concluding that he is in a state of "apathy." The *fact* of the matter is that the cry has stopped him dead in his tracks, in the very midst of desperate action. Shakespeare knows well enough that a certain kind of man will tell himself many things, not because they are true, but because he would prefer to believe them; and Macbeth has been painstakingly and persistently set before us as precisely that kind of man. What his speech *expresses as an action*—as op-

116

posed to what the words *say*—is the feeling that he has already suffered so much terror and anguish that he thought he could suffer nothing more; and yet, here is more.

At this point he is told that his queen is dead. He says, "She should have died hereafter."

I must reject the view of G. B. Harrison that this means "She would have died at some time or other," together with the late G. L. Kittredge's very similar view:

Macbeth receives the news of his wife's death with apathy, and does not even ask the manner or the cause. 'Ah, well, she would certainly have died *some* time!'

Why on earth should he ask the manner and the cause? Doesn't he *know* the cause? Hasn't he, two scenes before, described it in detail to the Doctor? Doesn't he have more intimate knowledge of it even than that, as the ill about his own heart? Can he have much doubt about the *manner* of her death? In any case, would these questions proceed from deep grief, or from impertinent and unfeeling curiosity?

He gives the reason for what he has said, and its meaning too, in the very next line: "There would have been a time for such a word." Her death is a disaster; this is no time for further disasters; he cannot endure any more just now. This is, like Lady Macbeth's sign, the expression of a heart that is "sorely charged." The point is missed completely by E. K. Chambers:

I think that this line can only be taken as an expression of Macbeth's callous indifference to everything but his own danger. His wife's death arouses no emotion; it only suggests a general reflection on the transiency of things.

Is that what we are to make of the terrible lines that follow? Are they an unemotional utterance of a "general reflection"? Can we possibly maintain that they proceed from "no emotion"? Must we have rant and noise to express abject grief? Is not despair a very quiet thing?

This is not general reflection at all: it is a particular character in a particular frame of mind, following a particular train of thought. Macbeth has said "*hereafter*": that is a word which has some particular meaning for him. It was the beginning of his whole tragedy: "All hail, Macbeth, that shalt be king hereafter!" He had written of it to his wife; on his return from war, her first greeting to him had been, "Great Glamis! Worthy Cawdor! Greater than both, by the all-hail hereafter!" and she had gone on to say, "Thy letters have transported me beyond/ This ignorant present, and I feel now/ Thy future in the instant."

Hereafter, which could then be made into a *tomorrow*, if the king died that night. He *did* die, and Macbeth presently was elected king; and yet there were always further tomorrows to be won, when he might have peace and safety. He has striven throughout to ensure the safe *tomorrow*; he talks throughout the play in terms of guarantees and contracts which will ensure it. He will cancel the great bond (of Fate with Banquo) which keeps him pale, he will take a bond of fate, he will live the lease of nature, he even com-

118

municates this notion to his wife, who says of Banquo and Fleance, "But in them Nature's copy (copyhold) 's not eterne." Others had expected tomorrows: Duncan, who had proposed to ride forth, and Banquo, who had thought to discuss with Macbeth on tomorrows that Macbeth knew would never come for them. Tomorrow now holds nothing for Lady Macbeth. And for Macbeth himself, who had once said, "Come what come may/ Time and the hour runs through the roughest day"—to a better tomorrow—tomorrow and hereafter mean little more than that "There would have been a time for such a word."

Hereafter is a succession of tomorrows, that come ever so slowly to those who await them with hope; each in turn becomes a today and shows that the hope was vain, and then becomes a yesterday. We hope, but the whole past tells us not to: all our yesterdays have only lighted fools—the fools, the dupes, of hope—on their way to death. Each day is a brief candle by which we live; let it go out, then, let there be no more such tomorrows, for the hope that they hold is vain. Macbeth's despair is so complete that he cannot imagine any life as different from his own; therefore life is a mere shadow, though it seems to be real, and all action is only the motion of a shadow. It is worse than that; for *we* think our actions meaningful and real (and there the horror lies) whereas we are only players moving briefly in a mockery of life and action, to an eventual silence. It is worse even than that: a play has a story with meaning behind it; whereas life is a tale meaningless in itself, accompanied by wild and meaningless sounds and gestures. And it is hope and tomorrow and hereafter that have deceived us into thinking otherwise.

This is the Macbeth who had said falsely, as he came from the bedchamber of the King he had murdered:

> Had I but died an hour before this chance,
> I had lived a blessed time; for, from this instant,
> There's nothing serious in mortality:
> All is but toys; renown and grace is dead;
> The wine of life is drawn, and the mere lees
> Is left this vault to brag of.

It is one of the many ironies in this play that he is here speaking truly, although he thinks he is feigning; and that he is to say this once more, in the speech we have been considering, from the bottom of his heart, and in saying it, to abandon all hope. For he does not hope after this; his actions subsequently are merely acts of desperation. True, he is immediately after this aroused by the sight of the Messenger, and stirred into action by the news that Birnam Wood has come to Dunsinane; but it is the desperate action—the crucial military mistake—of abandoning the castle and rushing upon his fate in the field. He has begun to be "a-weary of the sun," and has one comfort left: "At least we'll die with harness on our backs." And he fights, without hope, on the one assurance which Fate has left him, till that too proves false. If you can find hope here for him, you are welcome to it: I call it mere doggedness.

On the interpretation which I have outlined, the speech becomes an important event: it constitutes the termination of the hope which has been the mainspring of Macbeth's action throughout the play. And, whether you accept this interpretation or not, the speech certainly expresses Macbeth's state of mind. The speech produces a profound effect upon the stage. Is it because of the profundity of its ideas?

I do not think its ideas profound. As a matter of fact, I do not even think they are true. Life is meaningless, life is a sham, life is not worth living; these are familiar enough remarks to us, and they usually come from people we had rather not be familiar with. We associate them with the callow, the jejune, the superficial, the malcontent or simply silly people of the world, and disregard them. And I will entertain no objections here that such ideas are rendered profound by beautiful language and verse. If poetry can deceive us into thinking silliness profundity, I will gladly help Plato to kick it out of his or any other Republic. For it seems to me indeed then the enemy of truth.

Are there any cases in which such remarks could be meaningful and moving? Why, yes: when they are said by certain kinds of persons, who have been through certain experiences, and who are in certain circumstances. Suppose a man of the finest character, blessed with every good fortune, and active in every good way, confesses to you that he has found life meaningless; or suppose that one who you know has hitherto found great meaning in it tells you, after a certain event, that life has become meaningless. You find very different significances in one and the same remark, I believe, and you will be moved differently by them. But it will not be in the statement itself that you will find the significance; it will rather be in the fact that such and such a person should have uttered it in such and such a situation.

It is the same in the present instance. Shakespeare is not saying that life is a tale told by an idiot; he is saying that a man like Macbeth, who had done and suffered what Macbeth has, and who was in Macbeth's present situation, would say so. That is a very different thing. The profundity here is not Macbeth's but Shakespeare's. The speech has its significance and power in its manifestation of character and emotion.

Once again, then, we find dialog to be primarily a matter of signs. But surely the words themselves, the forms of expression, and the verse must matter somewhat? They matter very much indeed; but we must remember that the greatness of *Macbeth* as a *play* survives translation, and that it therefore cannot be due to the language or the verse. It must, then, reside in what is translatable; and what is translatable is precisely the *whole dramatic conception* which underlies language and verse. Certainly the diction and the verse permit a fuller and more refined expression of that conception; but we must not set the development and refinement above the elements which give the work its greatness.

And yet how marvelous these refinements are! Consider the last five lines again:

> Life's but a walking shadow, a poor player
> That struts and frets his hour upon the stage
> And then is heard no more; it is a tale
> Told by an idiot, full of sound and fury,
> Signifying nothing.

Here we have a series of metaphors for life, and each metaphor is also an image. A metaphor is a figure of speech; but we must remember that underlying it is a human being who, because of what he thinks and feels, sees one thing as resembling another, and who finds such meaning in the resemblance that he can call the one thing by the other's name. Underlying metaphor, therefore, are the probabilities of character, thought, and emotion; and wherever emotion is very intense, the imagination is stimulated to make images. We imagine very vividly whatever strongly arouses our hope, our fear, our desires and aversions; and these images incorporate whatever aspects make the thing in question an object of desire or aversion. When these are captured in words, the words themselves produce a similar image, and consequently a similar emotion, in those who hear or read them. As Longinus knew, an image can be a concealed argument of great persuasive power.

Now, this speech is no mere declamation, no mere aria for the star, no mere general reflection; it is part of the overwhelming *anagnorisis,* the Discovery-scene, of the tragedy. Macbeth is a man to whom prophecy has indicated that Fate will grant him some things and deny him others: he will have what is granted, he will bring it to pass by his own action, and he will contend with Fate, in the hope that he will also win what it has denied him:

> Rather than so, come Fate into the lists,
> And champion me to th'utterance!

That is, rather than that Banquo's issue should have the crown for which I killed Duncan, lost my peace of mind, and damned my eternal soul, let Fate itself come as a champion against me, meet me face to face, and fight to the death—*à l'outrance*.

This is the hope which dies in him at the news of his wife's death—the hope of altering the decrees of Fate. From here on, as I have said, he acts out of desperation, or if there is any hope, it is only the hope that Fate will abide by its promises. What can have killed that hope in him? He has known that his posterity cannot inherit since the Show of Kings, and his blind rage at that discovery made him determine henceforth to make action follow immediately upon thought. But here is the end of the partner and instigator of his actions, who shared his hope; he is forced to contemplate those actions and their result. Contemplating them, he discovers two things of which, in all their action, his wife and he had been ignorant: the nature of the doer and the inevitable result of the doing—a result which hope had painted otherwise. He knows, and the knowledge breaks him.

In his terrible calm despair he sees the whole of the Future, to the Last Day, and the entirety of the Past. Death is the only end, all hope is vain, life is a mockery. His anguish is too profound for violence; only once is there a touch of it, in the passionate rejection: "Out, out, brief candle!" The man who murders his own nature becomes a ghost, a walking shadow; the man who builds on vain hopes is a poor player in a mere pretense of action, whose very noise is soon silenced; the man who takes folly for wisdom, and falsity for truth, makes his life an unmeaning tale.

We contemplate these images and learn what it is to think so, and to feel so; and the beautiful verses tell

124

us of the tediousness of the coming of time, to both hope and despair, and of passionate rejection, and at last, in ever-lengthening cadences as the man sees deeper and deeper into himself, the dreadful silence which settles about the damned.

V
Emotion, Fiction and Belief

OUR DISCUSSION has led us to think of drama in a particular way. A plot—an action of some emotional power, and unified by some principle—is invented; a scenario indicates the order and nature of the actions to be represented by the actors; and speech or dialog both extend the possibilities of representation, and act upon us as words and their rhythms may. If we think of the representation and dialog as a photographer's filters, we can say that the plot comes to us, and affects us emotionally, first as filtered through the representation and second as filtered through the dialog.

A poor analogy, doubtless; yet I can think of no other way to put this. What I have in mind is that obviously the events of a plot do not always have the same effect upon us that they would in life itself. They may have a greater effect, or a lesser, or even an effect contrary to that which their natural counterparts would produce. That is, the representation can, so to speak, intensify certain colors, weaken others, block out others entirely and even replace them with a contrary hue; and the dialog can do much the same thing with the colors transmitted to us by the representation. The audience sees the plot through the dialog and the representation.

And of course, seeing it, the audience feels its effect. We have talked a good deal about that "effect"; we have assumed, and will continue to assume, that it is precisely in order to achieve this effect the whole work is organized and that this effect is what gives the work its value. A work somehow produces an effect upon an audience; well and good. But what do we mean by "effect?" And what is the mechanism, specifically, by which it is produced? And what sort of people have we in mind when we speak of the "audience"?

To take this last point first: we talk perpetually of the "delightful," the "painful," the "pitiable," the "venerable," and so on; but we need have very little experience of human nature to know that different people react differently; that what one man delights in gives another pain, that one pities or venerates what another does not. There are people who will laugh at nothing, and there are people who will laugh at everything. There are people who can sympathize with no one, and people who can sympathize with everyone. There are people who take a particular pleasure in what would distress most of us, and there are people who are greatly distressed by what most of us find pleasant. A little reflection on this incredible variety of human response, and we are likely to look with some melancholy on the critics who talk of works that have "pleased all men in all ages."

Indeed, we may say flatly that if the "audience" in-

cludes anyone and everyone, the dramatist is pretty
well out of business. He cannot write comedy, because
what strikes one spectator as funny will strike another
as very sad. He cannot write tragedy, because what one
takes as tragic another will laugh at. And so, drama is
impossible. Happily, the moment we reach this interesting conclusion, we see a way out. The dramatist
does not write for all men, he writes for a certain audience.

But what sort of audience? Baseball games are played
for those who like baseball, and football games for
those who like football. Shall we say that drama is for
those who happen to like drama, and let it go at that?
I think we must hedge a bit here and say, *Yes and No.*
No, if we let it go at that; *Yes,* if we push it farther. We
cannot simply define the audience of drama as one
composed of people who like drama. Baseball and football demand for their enjoyment merely a knowledge
of the game and a liking for it—assuming, of course,
the capacity to perceive what is going on. That "liking"
is in a sense accidental; that is, it has nothing to do
with the normality or abnormality, the presence or
absence of a moral sense, or any other characteristics
of the people who happen to have it.

The case of the dramatic audience is quite different.
The proper audience of drama cannot possibly be ab-
normal. All the arts presuppose a perfection of the
sense which they address. No painter paints for the
blind or the color-blind or for those of extremely dis-
torted vision; no composer addresses the deaf or the
tone-deaf or those without some rhythmic sense. Similarly, all the arts presuppose a perfection of more

than sense-perception. Tragedy, for instance, does not address those who take pleasure in the infliction of pain, like the sadist or masochist, any more than it does those who suffer hyperaesthesia; it addresses those of normal or better moral vision, much as music is for those of normal or better hearing.

We cannot, however, rush to the other extreme, and suppose that the proper audience of drama is ideal mankind—that is, people possessed of absolute virtue. In the first place, that might leave the theatres somewhat empty. Second,—while I do not know much about the point of view of the absolutely virtuous person—the saint or the true Philosopher after Plato's pattern may well take such lofty views of life that human mirth and anguish, as most men conceive these, become insignificant. There is some truth, doubtless, in Strindberg's observation in his preface to *Miss Julie:*

. . . Perhaps a time will arrive when we have become so developed, so enlightened, that we can remain indifferent before the spectacle of life, which now seems so brutal, so cynical, so heartless; when we have closed up those lower, unreliable instruments of thought which we call feelings, and which have been rendered not only superfluous but harmful by the final growth of our reflective organs.

I do not look forward with any eagerness to such a future condition of humanity; indeed, I take some comfort in the fact that it still seems as remote as it did in Strindberg's day. But it is not impossible; and if it should ever come to pass, drama—at least drama as we know it—will doubtless cease to exist.

Our argument seems to push us to the conclusion

that the proper audience of drama lies in a middle ground between the bestial and the godlike, the sub-human and the superhuman. Even here, however, we cannot admit everybody. Drama exhibits people of different kinds and of different moral character, doing such things as such people would be likely to do; hence the proper audience of drama must have some moral sense and some experience of humanity and human fortune or misfortune. They must have some ability to interpret the signs of emotion and character, and as much human feeling as will permit concern for the fortunes of others. Children, for example, can be too young and inexperienced to know what is probable in character and action, or to interpret signs. My own youngest children thought *The King and I* a very frightening movie, and the King a very bad man, simply because Yul Brynner spoke so loudly most of the time. The matter of "human feeling" is of course a variable one; I mean to imply that it must be active in the spectator throughout the performance.

The drama, like the novel, presents us with the fictitious fortunes of fictitious characters, and, as we saw far back in our discussion, with these precisely *as* fictitious. Obviously, then, what is exhibited cannot possibly be to our real or apparent advantage or disadvantage, and consequently cannot engage our self-interest. Not merely is self-interest not involved, but to the extent that it becomes involved, it must render the spectator incapable of proper response to the play. Could Macduff be present at a performance of *Macbeth*, his reactions would hardly be those at which Shakespeare aimed.

The proper audience of drama in general is thus composed of persons who can interpret and judge correctly of human behavior when this is presented *entirely apart from their self-interest*. Since self-interest is one of the factors principally responsible for the clouding and distortion of moral judgment, even ruthless and wicked people can respond properly to drama. History is full of tales of tyrants who have been pitiless to the reality but who have pitied the fiction. Plutarch's twice-told tale of Alexander Phaereus is one of many instances. Specifically, the various kinds and levels of drama demand different things of their audiences. Some require more intelligence and experience, greater moral sensitivity, and higher moral values than others. Children's plays, slapstick, and melodrama clearly demand less of their audiences than the higher forms.

I have spent this much time discussing what may seem unimportant, perhaps even obvious, because we are investigating the conditions of emotional response, and because it makes all the difference *whose* responses we are investigating. Every emotion comes into being through the concurrence of several factors. As we have seen, people feel different emotions according as they are of different character and disposition; but they do so also as they are in different frames of mind, or as their emotions have different objects, or as they contemplate different aspects or qualities of these. To say this differently: if you are trying to arouse fear in a given man, you will have to know what sort of man he is, what frame of mind he is in, what kind of thing he will fear, and precisely what he will find fearful in that thing. An object which is fearful to a man in one frame of mind will not necessarily be so to one in an-other; a man contemplating certain aspects of a given object may react differently from a man contemplating certain other aspects of it; and so on.

We may say, thus, that what particular emotion will be aroused depends upon four factors: *character or disposition, frame of mind, object,* and *aspect of the object.* It is perfectly possible, however, that in a given man, any one of these may be sufficient to cause the emotion. A man suffering from *Angst* will be apprehensive at anything and everything; a man in the frame of mind of Macbeth immediately after Duncan's murder will be appalled at every sound; certain objects, or certain aspects of these, evoke the same emotion in everyone.

The dramatist has no control over the kind of people who will see or read his play; he must assume the kind of audience we have already described, that is, one already of a certain character and disposition. The other three factors are very much within his control. He can put his audience into the frame of mind most conducive to a given emotion, and he can invent an object which can cause it, and emphasize those qualities or aspects which are particularly productive of that emotion. For instance, we are more prone to feel fear when we already feel a certain uneasiness, and the dramatist can promote that uneasiness by developing circumstances in which a terrible thing may very well happen: an isolated place where no one is likely to intervene, a time which is especially opportune for the thing to happen, persons especially liable to become victims of it, and perhaps already in some anxiety about it, and so on. He can also make the event as terrible as he wishes, and dwell precisely upon those aspects which make it terrible.

An emotion is a mental state attended by pleasure or pain. We can distinguish, I think, three different kinds of these. Some are pains; some are pleasures; some are desires or aversions. Pity is a pain which arises at the sight of some undeserved misfortune; fear is a pain which arises from the opinion that some dangerous thing is about to happen to ourselves or those for whose welfare we have some concern. Joy, hope, and mirth are pleasures; but emotions like anger are neither pleasures nor pains, but desires involving both pleasure and pain. I am assuming that we mean by anger a desire for retaliation, brought about by some painful thing inflicted upon us, and sustained by the pleasurable expectation of achieving retaliation; it thus involves both pleasure and pain.

Emotions are *caused,* as we have seen, by the concurrence of four factors; and they are *dispelled,* in general, by the removal of whatever causes have been operating. If you pity someone, I can dispel that pity by convincing you that the person is suffering in no way, or that such pain as he is suffering is far less than he deserves; I can modify it by some depreciation of his suffering, or some augmentation of his guilt; I can even turn your pity into another emotion entirely (let us say, fear) by convincing you that the same thing is immediately going to happen to *you.*

I can hardly embark here upon a full discussion of the emotions, nor am I competent to do it. These are matters for the psychologist. But look for them in

134

Aristotle, or Spinoza, or Hobbes, or Locke, or Hume; modern psychologists, so far as I know, no longer occupy themselves with distinguishing the various kinds of emotion as accurately as possible. The contributions of modern psychology are doubtless very great; I must confess, however, that I find it all but useless to the artist or student of art who must know as minutely as possible just what kind and degree of emotion is being aroused.

Indeed, to have such knowledge we should have to know a good deal more than the nature of fear, joy, and the rest of the list. These are not single emotions, but rather whole families of emotions, and the family resemblance is not always great. *Fear,* for example, includes everything from simply being startled to being mad with panic; and *anger,* everything from annoyance to rage. Yet some of the forms of fear bear little resemblance to each other; the paralysis of extreme dread is a quite different feeling from frantic fear.

Our bodily conditions, our sensations, our memories, images of our imagination, our thoughts and opinions, even our emotions themselves all produce emotions within us. Sickness and fatigue, for instance, immediately cause certain mental feelings; a loud noise startles, perhaps even terrifies. The effects of memory, imagination, and opinion upon the emotions are obvious to everyone. Even emotion produces emotion, as I have just said: I am afraid and ashamed because I am afraid, I am angry and confident because I am angry. Of all these sources of emotion, only the first is beyond the control of the dramatist; but if he has no control over our real bodily conditions as such, he can place us in imaginary ones. More importantly he can determine what we shall see and hear; he can induce us to recall earlier portions of the play; he can operate upon our imagination and opinion.

The fact that the dramatist, unlike other writers, works directly upon our sensations gives his art a peculiar vivacity and force. At the same time, perhaps no literary art is so dependent upon inference as drama. Poetry and fiction tell us directly about the characters and their actions and feelings, and interpret them to us constantly; the dramatist simply sets them before us, and we must interpret for ourselves. Usually we must infer the identity of the characters, their situations, their moral characters, their relations to one another, their motives, passions, even many of their actions, and a good deal beside.

Indeed, a very little reflection will show us that the dramatic audience is constantly engaged in inference, and that inference is the principal mechanism producing our impressions and emotions. The audience is not usually *aware* that it is constantly inferring, for two reasons: it is too much occupied with its emotions, and the whole process of inference is so habitual that it takes place without any particular consciousness of it, for people infer constantly in daily life. We form an opinion of someone's situation or character, on the basis of a look, a remark, an act, without reflection on the fact that this is inference. Similarly, there is constant inference in drama; for as we have seen, the very possibility of drama is based upon signs, and inference is what follows upon these. The best way to establish the fact of inference is to pay some attention to yourself during a performance; you are constantly observing this or that, inferring from what you observe that the characters are people of a certain kind, in certain situations, or that such and such an event has happened or is likely to happen, and so on. Unless you are watching very crude drama indeed, you will be told little directly. In one respect inference is even more important than sensation; for you can gain some idea of a play by reading it, but a person unable to infer would get very little indeed even from witnessing a performance.

Put it this way, then: we infer, and as a consequence, frame opinions which are the conclusions of our inferences; and these opinions lead us to feel various emotions. When opinion functions at all in emotion, it is likely to be decisive. If I have the opinion that something is dangerous I shall fear it, whether it is in fact dangerous or not; conversely, if I have the opinion that it is not dangerous, I shall not fear, regardless of the actual fact. The plot is what is revealed to us; the representation and the dialog are the instruments of revelation, and determine point by point what the materials of inference shall be, and consequently what opinions we are to frame and hence what emotions we shall feel. Consider what a dramatist reveals or conceals as the play proceeds, how much in consequence the audience knows or does not know, what it will or will not conjecture, and to what at any moment its attention is particularly directed; you will then be able to say with some precision what emotions it will feel, and when. The audience will, for example, feel a given emotion precisely at the point where it makes the inference which leads to the emotion. In a drama or novel the principal emotions are aroused by the nature of the characters and of their fortunes, past, present, or future, and the principal inferences, consequently, will be those concerning characters and fortunes. Moreover, one emotion will change into another as there is some change in one or another of the three factors of emotion—in, that is, the frame of mind, or the object of emotion, or the particular aspect of the object; and it is possible thus to trace the transmutation of one emotion into another.

Emotions are increased in degree through suspense or through surprise. Suspense is anxiety caused by extended anticipation, and hence, either by the uncertainty of something we wish to know, or by prolonged waiting for something to happen. A child is in the first kind of suspense until he learns what he will get for Christmas; then he remains in the second kind of suspense until he actually gets it. Both kinds must involve something which is desirable or undesirable, about the existence or nature of which there can be some uncertainty: we can never be in suspense about something which is absolutely indifferent to us, or about something which is inevitable or impossible. Suspense is increased by unexpected frustration, so long as the anticipation of further frustration does not ultimately make the outcome indifferent to us.

All emotions are greater if produced immediately from their contraries: for instance, fear is greater in one who has just been confident, and greater still in someone who has just been more confident. Surprise and the unexpected effect just this; they always produce a certain degree of shock. The greatest surprise comes about when the thing which happens is not only unexpected but contrary to expectation, and when that expectation itself is as strong as possible. If you expect me to do something nice for you, and I do not do it, you will of course be surprised; you will be even more surprised if I do you harm instead; and in each case the degree of surprise will be in proportion to the strength of your expectation.

Suspense and surprise may seem more suitable to melodrama than to more serious forms; but this is by no means the case. The greatest drama has always used them with particular power, and so have the greatest novels. They are devices which may amount to little when used for their own sake; but when used to higher ends, they can produce overwhelming effects.

There are a few other questions that we must pursue before we can leave this topic of emotion. First of all, why should the events of drama affect us as they do? What produces the laughter or the horror or the pity? I must respond: the laughable, the horrible, the pitiable, in art precisely as in life. I can take no stock in a supposed "aesthetic reaction" which is entirely peculiar to art and which involves emotions different from those we feel outside the sphere of art. We are the same persons, we cannot really alter, whether we are reacting to art or to reality.

But how is it, then, that pleasure can result from the representation of tragic, even sordid, events which, if real, would harrow or disgust us? In Hume's words, "It is certain, that the same object of distress, which pleases in a tragedy, were it really set before us, would give the most unfeigned uneasiness." Hume's solution of this problem is that eloquence, imitation, and the predominant pleasurable passion which arises from imitation work together to transmute the painful into the pleasant. I think this is true, but perhaps not the whole story.

It is not a matter for argument, it is plain fact, that we are emotionally moved by fictions, that these fictions contain many things naturally unpleasant or even painful, and that nevertheless we enjoy being moved as we are, so that the naturally painful becomes pleasant. We might easily conclude, on these grounds, that nothing could be more absurd than the statement that the laughable, the horrible, the pitiable in life are identical with their counterparts in art. If fear is a pain and the naturally fearful object becomes pleasant when depicted in art, patently it cannot arouse real fear, or fear at all; for a species of pain can never be a species of pleasure. We might press this view so far as to claim that all things, whatever their natural effect, become pleasant simply through being imitated, and that there is thus a complete separation between art and nature.

But the case is not so simple. It is also fact that the arts do evoke painful emotions in us—a thing which would be impossible on hypotheses just presented. What is more, when the emotion is extremely intense, people are sometimes deceived into taking the illusion for reality. When that happens, pleasure is instantly supplanted by pain. A good number of women faint during the horrific performances at the Grand Guignol Theatre; their agitation, pleasurable up to a point, apparently reaches such an extreme that it becomes painful. Does a phenomenon of this sort indicate that the difference between pleasure and pain is a matter of degree? And that, as Fontenelle thought, a mild fear produces pleasure, whereas an extreme degree of fear produces pain? I should say rather that fear, mild or violent, is in any case a painful emotion; that pain is pain, and pleasure, pleasure, and that neither can really *become* the other.

Perhaps we can solve these problems by asking a number of questions. Let us assume, first of all, what I have already proposed: that we do not feel, in the presence of art, emotions actually distinct from those we feel in life—that is, we do not feel an emotion X through art which could not possibly be felt except through art. Let us assume, too, that there is a natural correspondence between the emotions produced by art and those produced in nature: that is, that the emotion of fear we feel at a play is the same emotion which we call fear in life and due to the same general causes.

We may now ask: Does the fictitious incident differ from the real one in the *degree* of emotional quality? Is a fearful one less fearful, or a pathetic one less pathetic? I think the answer is obvious. Certainly not. Imagine a catastrophe as dreadful as possible; it will be just as dreadful, in itself,—and no more or less so— if it happens exactly as imagined. Similarly, a fictitious hero is no less heroic, a fictitious villain no less villainous, than a real one, and good or evil fortunes are no less good or evil in *themselves* because they are imaginary rather than real.

But does the fictitious when known to be fictitious

affect us exactly as the real? No. When we react emotionally to purely imaginary events, we respond to an idea or image of some good or bad fortune *in itself;* or to it as happening to a certain kind of person, or a particular person, and thus *in relation.* Imagine, for example, the destructive powers of an earthquake or a hurricane; as you imagine these, you will instantly respond with certain emotions. Now imagine these as affecting persons of different moral character, persons more or less deserving of sympathy or antipathy, persons immediately or remotely connected with you. Now your original emotions will be in some way qualified, perhaps altered entirely, as you conceive the events as affecting different persons. Now suppose the imagined event to become real; plainly your reactions will be affected by the additional reflection that it is real.

But this is an *additional reflection.* The differences between our reactions to fiction and our reactions to reality must be wholly due to this reflection, since it constitutes the sole difference between the fictional and the real which can affect our thought or belief. So far, then, from our response to fiction being a matter of "willing suspension of disbelief," as Coleridge thought, no disbelief arises or is suspended, nor is volition involved at all. The fiction has simply not excited the additional reflection and the further responses attendant upon it, whereas the real considered as real inevitably must excite them. We respond to the imagined good or evil fortune, and to it as imagined to be happening to someone; and these are the most potent and important factors in our response. They are so even when the event is real; without them our response to reality itself would be feeble and in-determinate. Suppose I say to you, "Something really happened to someone; yes, it really did; how do you feel about it?" Just how *do* you feel? How can you feel anything at all, unless you know *what* happened to *whom?* What is more, your response even so will be relatively slight unless your imagination has been aroused. You read daily in your newspapers of events which you know are real—events sometimes of great emotional power—without particular excitement; and you remain unexcited because your imagination has not been stirred. On the other hand, you suffer many emo-tions—worry, hope, fear, and so on—knowing per-fectly well that the object of your emotion is im-aginary, for it has not yet happened. Another point: if a play has failed to interest or excite us, we are not much moved on learning that it depicted real events. Conversely, if it has interested and excited us, it is no less interesting or exciting when we reflect that it is only fiction.

We see, thus, that the imagination supplies the very foundation of many of our emotional responses, even to reality itself. So far from wondering how we can respond to the purely imaginary, we might reflect that we should hardly react to reality as we do, were it not for the activity of our imagination. The fiction would not, if it became real, continue to affect us in the same way; on the other hand, if the real were viewed in the same light and with the same self-detachment as the fiction, it would affect us exactly as the fiction. The emotional power, as this argument has shown, resides primarily in the imagination; the additional reflection on its reality serves only to qualify or modify that power. Our reactions to fiction are not based upon the reflection that what we imagine is imaginary, but on the *absence* of the reflection that it is real. A play affects us, then, by providing us with images exactly of the status of images of the imagination. The fact that our senses are affected, that we actually see and hear, merely gives these images greater vividness and precision. It does not turn illusion into delusion so that these images are taken as real. We are aware that we are in the theatre, as Samuel Johnson thought; but our attention—if the play is a good one—is wholly given over to the dramatic image.

Still, we may ask, how does the painful produce pleasure? I think we can distinguish at least four ways in which this is possible. First, a painful emotion may produce a pleasant one directly. For example, pity produces benevolent feelings which are pleasurable; our friends are seldom so dear to us as when they suffer some misfortune, and our interest in and concern for the characters of drama is at its greatest when they are in adversity. Second, a painful emotion may lead indirectly to a pleasurable one. Our relief from pain is generally pleasurable in proportion to the degree of the pain from which we have been relieved; our pleasure in some achievement is proportional to the dangers and the difficulties which have been overcome. Third, a painful emotion may be a factor in a complex one which is pleasurable. We take pleasure in the courage of a brave man, and that exactly in such degree as the danger which he confronts is dreadful; without the painful emotion of fear the pleasurable one of ad-

144

miration would be impossible. Finally, even in painful emotions, there are often factors which, in and by themselves, are pleasurable. We see a tiger in the zoo and take pleasure in its size, its strength, its agility, its ferocity, the sharpness of its claws and fangs—all qualities which would fill us with horror, were we its prey. The power which would be a factor in the painful emotion of fear is here a cause of pleasure.

Obviously these considerations apply as much to fiction as to reality. Pathetic and sentimental novels and plays display the misfortunes of their characters, and so work upon the benevolent feelings of the audience. Tragedy and its narrative counterpart produce their special pleasure by the catharsis of, or relief from, painful emotions which have been aroused to a high degree. Adventure stories and melodrama excite fears so that the audience may enjoy the courage and prowess of the hero; the greater the danger and difficulty, the greater the excitement. Finally, certain kinds of horrific fiction and drama emphasize either the differences of circumstance or of character which set us apart from the dangers encountered, so that the fearful evokes wonder rather than fear.

All emotions depend upon certain conditions. If we may return to Coleridge's theory of the "willing suspension of disbelief for the moment, which constitutes poetic faith," I should like to remark that this by no means explains our reactions to fiction. On the contrary, to accept it is to make the explanation of emotion impossible. We *must* believe something, or we shall not feel any emotion at all. We need not believe that we are watching real events; in fact, as I argued much earlier, it is a condition of our proper response to drama that we positively should not believe this. But to say this is a long chalk from saying that disbelief is suspended. Except when it proceeds immediately from bodily sensations of pain and pleasure, emotion is dependent upon belief. How shall you produce fear in someone who does not believe anything is fearful? Or that anything can be painful or destructive? Or that, granted there are such things, there is any possibility of their happening imminently? What reaction can you expect from an audience which does not believe that there is any distinction between good and bad fortune, between good and bad character, between the signs which indicate these?

In short, the whole justification of probability and necessity of character and action—apart from the consideration that without these, imitation itself would be impossible—is that without them we should not believe, and without belief we should not be moved. *But,* the ghost of Coleridge says in my ear, *you are arguing that belief is requisite; I said the same thing; that is why I said* disbelief *should be suspended.* I remain cantankerous, however. We do not suspend disbelief. If we did, there would be no reason for probability or credibility. The fact is that we are as audiences very quick to notice improbabilities; consequently, we cannot be said to suspend disbelief. We do not even suspend disbelief that the fiction is reality, for if we did, it would strike us as no different from the real. We merely credit fiction to the extent that it is credible. This is a point which, if it is not clear to Coleridge, was perfectly so to Samuel Johnson.

146

The dramatic illusion has frequently been compared to a dream state. It can hardly be that, for in dreaming we generally accept the dream as reality. Rather it is akin to imagination, except that the whole process, with all its various images, is under the control of someone other than ourselves. And we respond to the emotional quality of the images precisely as images.

VI
Dramatic Effect and Dramatic Form

WE HAVE BEEN talking about emotion in a way that may suggest that it is the whole effect of drama, or the chief effect, or at least the distinguishing characteristic which sets one form apart from another. This is not quite the case. Emotion is unquestionably of great importance, but it is not so important as all that. Certainly it is not the whole effect. We have seen that emotion itself is produced in large part by activities of the intellect and the imagination. Without inference the audience cannot know what is going on, and consequently cannot respond to it. Without imagination it cannot feel hope, fear, suspense, or any emotion which involves either anticipation or memory. All such emotions have as their objects things not present to sensation, things that consequently must be imagined.

Indeed, however much aestheticians talk about them, such notions as a "purely emotional effect" or a "purely intellectual response" are chimeras. Philosophers have often and variously distinguished the mental faculties of man; but these are all distinctions of reason, and do not imply any real separation. *Myself as father* can be distinguished from *myself as husband, myself as teacher, myself as citizen;* but these are not really separate entities. They all exist together in one person, and what affects one affects all. The same thing is true of our faculties. No matter how they are distinguished in philosophical analysis, they are not watertight compartments. What affects reason affects imagination, what affects imagination affects emotion; in short, there is every sort of interplay. That interplay does not exist merely among the mental faculties; it exists also between body and mind. Bodily feelings, conditions, and activities work upon the mind; the mind works upon them. I have no great argument to offer here; I must simply ask you to look at the facts. And the salient fact is that we are involved, body and soul, in all that we suffer or do. People do use such expressions as "head but not heart," and the rest; but these are figurative expressions, metaphors. We are concerned with literal fact.

Emotion cannot, then, be the whole effect of drama or anything else. We respond in totality. But, while we respond in totality, it is possible that one faculty may be more active than another; and another look at the facts will assure us that this actually happens. If you are adding up a column of figures, your imagination and emotions are usually not much engaged, unless something of high emotional interest—such as bankruptcy or the detection of embezzlement—depends upon the answer. If you are extremely angry you are usually insensitive to the pain of a blow. In short, what we are intent upon, what we are engrossed in, seems to make all the difference.

150

It would seem plausible, thus, at first sight, that emotion might be the primary or chief effect of drama. And this seems, too, to be borne out by the strong emotional excitement which we feel, the way in which we praise a play as "very moving," the way in which we tend to distinguish different dramatic forms through their emotional effects, and a good many other considerations. Even so, emotion cannot be the chief effect of drama. Let us suppose that the end or chief effect of a certain kind of drama is fear. Fear in *whom?* Fear at *what?* What kind of *fear?* Obviously—even if we put in all the qualifications about the dramatic audience which we explored in the preceding chapter— there is still a very considerable range of things that may be feared and of persons who may fear. What frightens a child may not frighten an adult, what frightens a savage may not frighten a civilized man, what frightens an ordinary man may not frighten a man of exceptional character. Now, any drama, in order to produce fear, must propose some object as fearful, and in so doing assumes as its audience persons to whom it will be fearful. Emotions are in general common to all men; we think that everyone, whatever his character and quality, feels anger, grief, joy and so on, and nobody is better or worse simply because he feels such emotions. But the moment we talk about the *objects* which evoke these emotions, the case is entirely different. To say what specific object causes a given emotion is at once to indicate the character of the person who feels it, to exhibit what he regards as desirable or undesirable, pleasant or painful, good or bad. We begin immediately to make moral evaluations: morbid fear, silly fear, cowardly fear, petty wrath, irrational anger, noble rage, and so on.

Evidently, then, the emotion of drama can never be emotion *simply;* it must be emotion as proposed to give satisfaction to someone of a certain character, whether good or bad. And we tend to judge various kinds of drama according to the kinds of audience which they address: this piece is mere pornography, this is morbid, this is infantile, this is sublime tragedy. In all such judgments there is a point, established by moral principle or by moral convention, which marks a distinction between the acceptable and the odious, and there are similar points similarly established which mark the distinctions between what is acceptable or not to a given class. For example, children's plays are not morally odious, but do not commonly satisfy adults.

Emotions are also not peculiar to any given form, although we usually speak as if they were. Aristotle himself seems to have given some support to this notion by his remark that pity and fear are peculiar to tragedy. I do not think he means what he appears to mean; however, Aristotle or no Aristotle, the facts say otherwise. Any dramatic form can and does arouse almost every sort of emotion. Pity and fear, for instance, are aroused not merely by tragedy, but by melodrama and certain sentimental forms as well. Indeed, they can be aroused even by comedy.

Thus the effect of drama must involve something more than emotion. What is that "something more"? It can hardly be called a formed state of character, such as disposes one to act habitually in a certain way. Drama and all other arts are sometimes practised very successfully by persons of doubtful character, and sometimes appreciated by persons of doubtful character. It is not even an ethical or moral condition as such, for these are always related to our own actions. Perhaps we can describe it as a pre-ethical condition; a condition of mind in which we allow our ethical values, whatever they may be, to operate freely, undisturbed by reflections upon our own actions or self-interest.

I am quite content to leave this side of the matter to the moralist or the psychologist. What interests me is that our emotions are evidently functions of a system of values, and are regulated by that system. These values are practical ones, of course; they have to do with pleasure and pain, good and bad, desire and aversion, what we take to be happiness and what we take to be misery; and whatever our particular system of values may happen to be, higher or lower, better or worse, we feel emotion in terms of it. We cannot hope or fear or rejoice or grieve without valuing something; and what we value, and how much we value it, determines the quality and degree of our hopes and fears and joys and griefs.

Every emotional experience must either confirm or alter in some way our system of values; and in altering it, make it better or worse whenever it affects a moral value. This must hold true, also, of drama and the other arts. Can the arts debase us? I am afraid that it is perfectly possible for them to do so. But that question seems to me to belong to a discussion entirely different from the present one. We have assumed an audience of some morality, and we need only consider

153

such kinds of art as would be addressed to such an audience.

On such assumptions we can broadly distinguish two kinds of art, and hence of drama. The first assumes the system of values of the person of ordinary morality. It proposes simply the arousing of emotions to the ultimate effect of giving pleasure. That is, its aim is entertainment. Its effect is transitory, and its excellence consists simply in the intensity of the pleasure which it gives. That intensity is naturally dependent upon the intensity of the emotions produced; thus the serious forms of this kind tend to play upon extreme fear and other painful emotions, while the comic forms play upon the extremer reactions of the ridiculous. Melodrama, pathetic drama, slapstick, "frothy" comedy— generally we expect no more and get no more from these than thrills and chills, a good laugh, a good cry.

The "view of ordinary morality" is a crude and superficial one. Character and action are taken at face value. The kinds of character are relatively few, they are easily distinguished as good or bad and of a certain degree of goodness or badness, the motives of action are few, simple, and obvious, and the moral quality of an action can be seen at once, for every act is what it seems to be and springs from exactly the motive we should have supposed, unless the author is deceiving us so that he may surprise us later. Character is almost reduced to circumstance: the murder is more horrifying if the victim is harmless, defenseless, and innocent; the custard pie gets more laughter if it hits the dignified dowager. The crudest generalizations about humanity often serve as probabilities of char-

154

acter and action. Negroes steal chickens, shoot craps, and are terrified of ghosts; Jews are rapacious and cunning; soldiers are brave; bullies are cowards, and so on. Intensity of effect is everything; and for the sake of that intensity, more enduring effects are foregone. The sensational forms—let us call them that—may sometimes haunt our imagination; or, if they are of high technical excellence, we may be drawn back to examine the craftsmanship. But commonly they merely entertain us, and we cannot come back to them with any pleasure unless we have in good part forgotten them. And, however much they entertain us, they leave us pretty much the same persons we were before we knew them. When I was a boy, Conan Doyle's *The Lost World* and certain books of Stevenson's, Verne's, and even John Buchan's enchanted me for many days. The illusive worlds which they created hung in my mind like colored mists that refused to be dispelled. I returned to them again and again, like the scholar to his Talmud, until I wore them out; I discussed them with my friends, and we made them the substance of our play. In short, the books had such effects on me as they have on every boy; but I do not think I can claim, even for such exceptional instances, that they changed me as a human being and made me otherwise than I should have been, or that they gave me any very penetrating or profound insights into human beings and their actions.

Not that they should have done so; indeed, had they done so, they could not have done what they did. The point is that certain novels and plays do, precisely, go beyond entertainment, and permit us perceptions which we should not otherwise have had; do go beyond ordinary morality, and offer us other and better systems of values; do, in some degree, alter us as human beings. *The Devil's Disciple* and *Captain Brassbound's Conversion,* for example, are very different from the melodramas which they parody, for they bring into question all the assumptions which underlie such melodramas. *Moby Dick* is something more than a tale of adventures in whale-hunting, and *Treasure Island* would have been a very different book if Melville had written it. What is the difference between *Moby Dick* and *Treasure Island?* It is not that one gives pleasure and the other does not. They both give pleasure; but there is a difference in the quality of the pleasure which they give. The pleasure given by *Moby Dick* seems to me superior to that given by *Treasure Island. Moby Dick* arouses emotions which imply an attitude somehow superior to that assumed by *Treasure Island.* Or, to put it differently, *Moby Dick* depends upon a superior sense of human values; that is, upon moral perceptions and evaluations (and emotions resulting from these) which require maturity, experience, and a good many other things from the reader. A boy can relish *Treasure Island* as much as, perhaps more than, an adult; I do not think that is true of *Moby Dick.*

There is a difference between having an experience simply and grasping the meaning of the experience. T. S. Eliot remarks in one of the *Four Quartets,* "We have had the experience, but missed the meaning." That is exactly the distinction I have in mind. The sensational forms give us the experience; the superior forms give us significant experience; and they are superior in the degree that the significance is a superior one. We judge authors, very properly I think, according to their perceptions of the meaning of experience, and the attitude which they induce us to take, by literary means, if we are also to perceive that meaning.

In these terms we can distinguish three levels of literary criticism. The first is that practised by any reader or theatre-goer: it involves nothing more than taking in the work and judging it as pleasing or displeasing. The second is that practised by most literary critics in their technical analysis: it involves ascertaining how the effect of a work is produced through certain technical causes. It can tell us about the craftsmanship of the work as good or bad; but it may quite possibly tell us that the craftsmanship of *Treasure Island* is, as pure craftsmanship, equal to or better than that of *Moby Dick*. The third kind of criticism is not technical; perhaps it is not even literary. It involves an assessment of the effect as effect, or, in other words, of the experience which we have in responding to the work precisely according to its value as an experience. This last kind of criticism must involve extra-literary, indeed extra-artistic considerations; for it must depend upon such values as we hold in life itself. We must invoke such values when we pronounce *Moby Dick* a greater book than *Treasure Island;* and we must practise such criticism because it is necessary to distinguish a *Moby Dick* from a *Treasure Island,* and because technical analysis in itself cannot do this. To practise the second kind of criticism one need merely be a critic, and he can be taught to do this; to practise the third kind with any success one must be a human being of a somewhat high order. Whether one can be taught to be such a being is a matter of some dispute.

To put this in a nutshell: there is a difference between works which give us an intense experience and works which give us a significant experience; there is a difference between a criticism which investigates the use of technical means toward a given end and a criticism which evaluates the end to which they are used. And it is to this latter criticism that we must turn if we are to settle problems of artistic form.

What is this meaning, this significance, about which I have been talking at such length? Certainly not the verbal meaning of sentences in the work. And certainly not some *moral* to be derived from the work, in the style of old-fashioned schoolteachers. The moral of *Othello* is that women should be careful how they bestow their linen, said Thomas Rymer, thinking of Desdemona's troubles with a certain handkerchief; we laugh at this, precisely because this moral—or any other—is so far removed from the significance of the play. Nor is it the meaning of the artificial or natural signs of which we spoke earlier; unless we grasped that, we should hardly follow the work at all, and besides, when we have grasped that, we can still fail to grasp the significance of the work. Indeed, the significance I have in mind *assumes* the proper interpretation of the work as a whole, and is something beyond it.

Is the apprehension of that significance a form of knowledge? If so, it is certainly not philosophic or scientific knowledge; otherwise we should all go into the theatre as ordinary persons and come out as philosophers and scientists. It is not even technical knowledge of the art of drama, or we should emerge as dramatic critics. It is not even practical wisdom, at least not in Aristotle's conception of *phronesis.* That is a virtue or formed state of character, and we are not actually made virtuous even by the highest and noblest art. *Phronesis,* too, comes from action and implies future action, whereas this apprehension does neither. It has this much in common, however, with practical wisdom: it is concerned with human affairs, and it recognizes particulars as well as universals. That is, it is not the discovery of the moral principle or precept involved, after the fashion of the moral-hunting pedagog, but the recognition that such and such a specific action *has* a certain moral quality.

It is clearly concerned with human action and passion, in such a view as is related to, but not identical with, that of practical wisdom. We suppose the man of practical wisdom to be a good judge of actions, and one who can see as deeply as need be into them, who can in adequate degree comprehend the motives and feelings and situations of those who act. He is thus a sympathetic judge, and one who can see action in all its relevant aspects with compassionate understanding. He sees both the causes and consequences of human action, and knows how circumstances alter cases. He can regard even the criminal with compassion, without permitting that compassion to affect his judgment of good and evil.

I shall say, therefore, that a work possesses significance or meaning as it promotes perceptions—perceptions based on feelings—which are conducive to practical wisdom; which would, if acted upon, eventuate in such wisdom. The condition of mind which it immediately promotes is a temporary alignment of passion, emotion, and desire with right principle.

From these considerations we can readily discern the absolute necessity of truth in fiction. There must be truth in the depiction of character and thought and emotion and action and of what is right and wrong, important and unimportant, and all such matters; in short, every truth except that of particular existence. That is a truth which is essential to history and to news reports. It has nothing to do with fiction. Even in that respect, however, fiction is not false: for as we saw much earlier, it does not affirm that it is particular fact. The poet and dramatist never claim the real existence of their characters, they merely pretend it.

We can observe, too, from this point of view, the sheer absurdity of saying that fiction neither affirms nor denies, or that it has its own ends apart from those of life. The end of fiction is not truth; but fiction which is art is impossible without truth, and without the constant assumption or affirmation of truth. The only thing which it neither affirms nor denies is particular existence; that, I have said, it merely pretends. The view that art has some end completely separate from life and reality should by now appear so silly that we need not discuss it.

With this, I can bequeath the whole question to some better philosopher than myself.

The most general distinction we can make among the forms of drama—as also among the forms of fiction and poetry—is that between serious and comic. That distinction has been discussed a great deal in the history of literary criticism, but for the sake of brevity I should like to bypass earlier discussion and simply offer my own view. There are, however, a number of pitfalls (quite chock-full of struggling critics, by the way) which we had better take some note of in advance. First of all, we must not suppose that the difference between serious and comic is a matter of a happy or unhappy ending. Many serious actions do not end unhappily, and some comedies do not have happy endings; it would be absurd to call the *Oresteia* a comedy because everything works out well in the end, or *Volpone* a tragedy because the principal character goes off to prison. Again, we must not suppose that the events as such make all the difference: you will find deaths, beatings, unhappy love, murder plots, and all such in comedy as well as in tragedy. And we must not suppose that comedy has an indissociable connection with laughter. Many forms of laughter—the hysterical, the insane, the malevolent, the scornful, to name only a few—have nothing to do with comedy, and some forms of comedy do not produce laughter. Comedy is not even coextensive with the ridiculous, although the ridiculous makes up a large part of comedy. The ridiculous can be an object of disdain or contempt, and these are not the reactions of comedy; besides, the comic includes actions and characters which are neither ridiculous nor even funny, but simply gay and witty.

The distinction between the serious and the comic is basically one of value; of value as reckoned in terms of benefit or harm. We take seriously anything which we are actively considering as very pleasurable or painful, good or bad, beneficial or harmful. Since anything of this sort is the object of very strong desire or aversion, it is also the object of intense hope or fear and similar violent emotions. When we take our own fortunes and actions seriously, we consider them as importantly related to our happiness or misery, or at any rate, to our extreme joy or grief. When we take seriously the actions or fortunes of other persons, we consider them as importantly related to the happiness or misery, joy, or grief, of those persons, in much the same way; except that now another factor is introduced, the degree of importance we assign to the persons in question. We do not take seriously anything which we regard as unimportant to the well-being of anyone, nor anything which happens to people for whom we feel no important concern.

The comic, on the other hand, grows out of the unimportant. Either we feel that the events are unimportant to the happiness of the characters, or we feel that the characters themselves are of no importance. Yet the comic is not, as Schlegel, Bergson, and others have assumed, the simple negative of the serious; it must be something more, or every bad serious play would be a good comic one, and conversely. It has some positive element, that is, which makes it comic rather than merely non-serious. The merely unimportant is generally uninteresting whereas comedy is interesting and diverting.

We can see into this matter a little more clearly if we contrast the serious with the comic in terms of such factors of emotion as we discussed in the preceding chapter. The frame of mind conducive to a serious emotion is one in which we already feel certain desires or aversions with sufficient strength to make the issue a matter of great consequence to us, and one of no certain outcome. Important things hang in the balance; consequently, we feel a certain uneasiness, agitation, tension, or at any rate, some degree of solemnity. The frame of mind conducive to comedy is the reverse. We do not feel any very strong desires; we are relaxed, in the expectation of pleasure and amusement; we are confident that nothing very important will happen, and that if it does, it will not be bad. We are prepared to be somewhat condescending to the good characters and somewhat indulgent to the bad, either because their virtues and vices are not very important ones, or because we feel that they cannot result in any real good or harm, or because they are improbable to the point where we do not believe in them.

The persons who are the objects of our serious emotions are those whom we think liable to great good or harm, or capable of doing these. Those who are the objects of comic emotions are in some way opposite. Their virtues or vices are either not important ones, or ones producing no very good or bad action or result, or fantastic exaggerations of which we remain incredulous.

We discover the same opposition between the aspects in which we regard serious and comic characters. The serious emotion always has as a part of its ground the importance of character, action, fortune; the comic, the unimportance of these.

Yet, as I remarked earlier, the comic is not merely

the non-serious or unimportant; the positive element which distinguishes it and gives it its peculiar effect is either infectious gaiety or the ridiculous. A comedy like *You Never Can Tell* does not depend so much upon our reaction to the absurdity of characters or events as upon the gaiety of amiable people having a lot of fun. It is quite distinct, thus, from plays like *Volpone* or *The Alchemist,* which depend upon the ridiculous. The ridiculous, if we accept Aristotle's account of it, is the painlessly bad or ugly; in any case, ridiculous people are inferior people, and this is at some remove from gaiety and amiability.

Serious plays, then, depend upon the augmentation of those values which give an action its importance; and comic plays depend upon minimizing these to the point where the amusing and the ridiculous can work upon us.

We have now, in effect, distinguished the serious and the comic as different attitudes toward persons and events—attitudes which the dramatist himself assumed, and built into his work in such fashion that the work has the power of imposing them upon the audience. Within these general attitudes, however, are contained many special ones; thus there are higher and lower orders of the serious, and of the comic as well. I have already remarked that the pleasure derived from a sensational work like *Treasure Island* is inferior to that derived from a tragic novel like *Moby Dick,* and that the reason for this is that the attitude assumed by the former is inferior to that assumed by the latter. Even among novels or plays which propose more than entertainment, however, there are the more serious and the less serious. A work which assumes a lower scale of values cannot have the potential seriousness of one which assumes a higher; or, to put this differently, a work cannot possibly have seriousness beyond the dignity of its underlying conception. *Point Counter Point,* for example, does not seem to me as serious as *The Brothers Karamazov,* because the characters and their actions and fortunes, even the universe in which conceivably they *might* have acted and suffered, are less valuable. *A Farewell to Arms* seems to me less serious still. In the same way, *The Second Mrs. Tanqueray* is less serious than *Othello,* and *Iris* is even less serious.

What is truly most serious, in other words, is what is most serious in the best judgment; what is serious in an inferior judgment is less serious to the degree to which that judgment is inferior. The dramatist who tries to evoke pity and fear at what are truly the most destructive and painful evils must deal with what the best judgment would conceive those evils to be, not with what the mean or the sordid or the base would conceive them to be. Similarly with goods: the true goods are those that in the best judgment are best. The dramatist who takes a lower view will produce a play that will be less serious. The lowest limit is the view of what I have called "ordinary morality." The writer who falls below that will be condemned as base or immature.

To make this a little clearer, we may take as an example a novel that appeared about a decade ago. It was intended to be a serious novel, and was advertised as such. The plot dealt with a poor and humble young man who ultimately achieves great wealth and social position. We are intended to regard him as a virtuous young man: his virtues are thrift, ambition, industry, decision, shrewdness, and hardheadedness. There are some obvious obstacles to his success, as well as some contests he must win over characters who are less thrifty, ambitious, industrious, and so on; but of course he triumphs, occasionally through tricks that strike us as a little dubious, although these are evidently admired by the author as indications of the highest genius. He moves from the humblest and most uncertain employment to partnership in the firm, and—since he marries the boss's daughter—there is little question that he will eventually be sole owner. Indeed, the author intimates that he will found a great commercial dynasty. My point is not the triteness of this tale but the quality of the values which it assumes. Happiness is conceived simply as the achievement of wealth and rank. Virtue is conceived simply as the qualities which enable the hero to achieve such happiness. Love itself is seen simply as a happy chance which permits a more rapid achievement of happiness. The sheer puerility of these conceptions is beyond belief. This is *below* ordinary morality. Even the man whose life is devoted to the achievement of wealth and rank does not really regard these as the highest things in life.

In a word, it makes all the difference what the author proposes as good and evil, virtue and vice, happiness and misery, or even what he denies them to be.

166

Marco Millions, for example, is a bitter denial of the very values which are affirmed by the novel I have just mentioned; and it has at least the seriousness of one who can look with pity and contempt upon men for whom these values are supreme. Yet the positive values upon which this superior view is founded are themselves less serious than they might be. Had Marco lived by these instead, his life still would have fallen somewhat short of what most of us take to be the best.

I am by no means arguing that everything should be in the grand style, or that writers should deal only with the noblest characters or the loftiest views. I am saying that we cannot, and as a matter of fact do not, evaluate literature in terms of craftsmanship simply; assuming perfect craftsmanship, we still evaluate works in terms of the ends to which craftsmanship is directed; that is, in terms of the value of the experience which we have had from them. These values are inevitably moral ones; yet to approach literature in terms of them is not to submit literature to moral *criticism,* for the values are here conceived, not as *ultimates,* but as *conditions* of a better or worse response. It is one thing to say, as the moral critics do, that literature must be moral because morality demands it. It is quite another to say that it must be so if it is to have an effect worth getting.

The writer may—and of course will—try for any effect he wishes. But whatever effect he tries for, he will have to depend upon certain values. He cannot pass off a boy's values as a man's, or a criminal's as those of a just man. And he will achieve, in the end,

167

only what his values will permit. A fine adventure story, a *Treasure Island*, is a valuable thing, but it is not so valuable as a *Moby Dick* . . .

We have come, I see, full circle.

The use of a given dramatic form is in some sense a proposal to elicit a given kind of response. To use a comic form is to propose to amuse; to use the tragic form is to propose the evocation of the tragic effect. Every form, like every device, has its peculiar powers and its peculiar limitations. The form which is chosen must be one capable of producing the proposed response, and the choice of a given form is thus the most important technical decision which a writer can make.

The making of an instrument capable of realizing a given dramatic conception is comparable to the making of an artificial organism which is to have a certain life and activity of its own, and supplying it with organs which shall function so that it may have that life and activity. If an organism is to move, it must have some means of moving itself; if it is to see, it must have eyes; if there is to be the activity, there must be the capacity; if there is to be the effect, we must supply the cause.

If the play, similarly, is to have its intended effect, it must be empowered to do so by the materials assembled in it and by the organization of these. There is organized matter, and there is that for the sake of which it was organized. To talk adequately about these is ultimately to define any dramatic form.

The chief problem of this book is the nature of tragedy. We began with materials and the possibilities of their organization, and we have been working our way toward some conception of the end toward which they were assembled and organized. We are in a position at this point to press, if we wish, to a definition of the tragic form. I prefer, however, to give the discussion a different turn: to examine what tragedy has been, in some notable instances, and to speculate what it might be.

So I shall say only that tragedy is drama which proposes the exhibition of an action of the utmost seriousness and the utmost significance. We may now consider how that seriousness and significance may be variously achieved.

VII
The Agamemnon

AGAMEMNON is the first play of the trilogy remaining
to us of what was originally a tetralogy. The tetralogy
consisted of three tragedies—*Agamemnon, The Libation-Bearers,* and *The Eumenides*—and a satyr play,
Proteus. Aeschylus drew his materials for the tragedies
from the legends of the House of Atreus. Most of us
have known these legends, in one form or another,
from childhood, but perhaps we may review them
briefly anyway. Atreus and Thyestes were the sons of
Pelops. Thyestes wronged Atreus' wife; in revenge
Atreus killed the children of Thyestes and served them
to Thyestes at a banquet; because of this barbarous
deed, Thyestes laid a curse upon the House of Atreus.
This curse affected the sons of Atreus, Menelaus and
Agamemnon. The former had his wife Helen stolen
from him by Paris, and the Trojan War followed. In
order to go to his brother's help at Troy, Agamemnon
took ship with his hosts; they were becalmed through
the hostility of the goddess Artemis; and Agamemnon
was forced to sacrifice his daughter Iphigenia to ap-
pease Artemis. The winds then brought the Argives to
Troy. After a ten years' siege Troy was taken, through

Odysseus' strategy of the Wooden Horse, and the victors set sail for their homes.

The *Agamemnon* begins when a watchman, after a year-long watch for the beacon fires which are to betoken victory, at last sees them. All is not well within the kingdom of Agamemnon. His wife Clytemnestra has formed a liaison with Aegisthus, the son of Thyestes; she wishes to kill Agamemnon, thus avenging Iphigenia; and Aegisthus also desires vengeance. On his return, Agamemnon is persuaded to enter the palace. Despite the warnings of the prophetess Cassandra, who had been forced to accompany the king as a captive, the Chorus of Elders does not intervene or give the alarm; for Apollo, who had given her the gift of prophecy, had also arranged matters so that no one should ever believe her. Agamemnon is murdered treacherously in his bath, and Cassandra is also slain. Clytemnestra appears before the Elders, boldly announces her crime, and proposes thereafter to rule with Aegisthus.

The Libation-Bearers opens at the tomb of Agamemnon. Orestes, the son of Agamemnon, having grown up in exile, returns to Argos and discloses both his identity and his purpose to his sister Electra. Apollo, through the Oracle of Delphi, has counselled him to avenge his father's death by killing Clytemnestra and Aegisthus. He accomplishes his revenge, and soon after is assailed by the Furies, the Eumenides.

The last play of the trilogy opens in the Courts of the Oracle of Delphi, but the scene shifts presently to Athens. Orestes, tortured by the Furies and mad with remorse, but never deserted by his counsellor Apollo, is at last freed of his madness. Athene founds the Court of the Areopagus; he is tried by it and acquitted and purged of his guilt. The curse of the House of Atreus is at last removed.

The English-speaking reader is likely to encounter some obstacles to his appreciation of Aeschylus, as you may remember I did. Aeschylus was so shortsighted as to write in ancient Greek, never guessing that many of us should thus be forced to read him in translation. Translations do not always catch what is said, and very seldom catch the *tone* in which it is said. We can see something of the possible variations in tone, even when the translators are all competent, by looking at a few translations of a single line. This is a line from the first Chorus of the play, used as a refrain in that Chorus:

ailinon, ailinon eipe, to d'eu nikato

Literally this means, *Sing the Linus-song, the Linus-song, but may the good prevail*. The Linus-song was originally the dirge sung in lament of the early death of Linus, brother of Orpheus and the son of Apollo and Urania. The term was, however, eventually generalized to mean any death-lament.

John Stuart Blackie translates:

> Sing woe and well-a-day! But still
> May the good omens shame the ill.

E. H. Plumptre turns it into:

> Wail as for Linus, wail, wail bitterly
> And yet may good prevail!

Robert Browning reads:

> Ah, Linus, say—ah, Linus, song of wail!
> But may the good prevail!

E. D. A. Morshead:

> Ah woe and well-a-day! But be the issue fair!

Gilbert Murray:

> Sorrow, sing sorrow; but good prevail, prevail.

Louis MacNeice:

> Cry, cry upon Death; but may the good prevail.

Richmond Lattimore:

> Sing sorrow, sorrow; but good win out in the end.

The translators are all good ones. They are all good Greek scholars, several of them even great ones; and they are all poets, one of them great, one or two excellent. Their versions all have something in common, which is certainly the meaning of the Greek. I have no desire to find fault with them in any way, and lack competence to do it in any case. But they are all up against the perpetual trouble of the Aeschylean translator: the problem of what constitutes the true English equivalent of the original in *every* aspect, and not merely so far as the meaning is concerned. And each has had to solve this in his own way.

The style of Aeschylus is a dignified, an exalted one. What is the high style in English? Some translators have thought it best exemplified by the King James version of the Old Testament; some, by Spenser; some, by Milton; one, at least, seems to have taken Tennyson as his model.

The plays of Aeschylus are in verse. What is the

174

verse most strictly resembling that verse in English? Rhymed? Unrhymed? Strictly metrical? Free-running?

These are questions which the translator must solve, but there is always a certain irony attached to their solution: that obtaining something as close as possible to the original always involves the importation of something which has nothing to do with the original. Granted, let us say, that the high style is Milton or the Old Testament, what do we do to Aeschylus when we make him speak like Milton or like a Hebrew prophet, so that Agamemnon goes to his death amid reverberations from *Paradise Lost* or the *Book of Job?*

On the other hand, the Greek put into plain English simply does not have the power and the quality of the Greek. Every translator must feel somewhat like the boy in Terence Rattigan's play, *The Browning Version*, who translated lines 1399–1400 somewhat as follows: "We wonder at your incredible, your shameless insolence, corrupt woman! that thus you boast over the bloody corpse of your husband." When the instructor points out that the Greek says simply "over your husband," the boy explains that "that isn't exciting enough." And he is quite right. The plain English isn't exciting enough, we must use some literary cosmetics, brighten Aeschylus up a bit, even though in the end we are likely to see, not his face, but our paint.

And there are difficulties beyond those of language. The Linus-song, for example, must have had very profound associations for the Greeks. Linus was a minstrel of great gifts, like his brother Orpheus, and his early death at the hands of Hercules apparently came to be, for the Greeks, the very type of tragic and premature death. Such associations we can hardly recapture. And perhaps differences of convention make it impossible for us to feel the deep religious horror of the Greeks at regicide, parricide, and incest, horrible as we may still consider these. The poet of a ninth-century German Biblical epic, *The Heliand,* transformed Christ into a Saxon king, the disciples into his vassals. We may flinch a little to see Christ (a Christ without humility and resignation) distributing gold armlets, or to see the marriage in Cana turned into high wassail in a Saxon hall; but the poet had a point. When the difference between cultures is wide there is sometimes the necessity to translate associations and conventions as well as words.

Fundamentally, however, I am concerned with our possible difficulties with Aeschylus as a playwright. The dramas require us to form a quite different notion of action, of what is a play, of what is dramatic, from the notions which centuries of English drama have naturally instilled in us. In the first place, we are conditioned by much of our drama to think of action as physical action, especially physical action of an exciting order. In a way, we unconsciously expect a play to be something like a prize fight, or a tennis match. We like deed following on deed, producing situation after situation, in quick succession; we like to look at these fairly superficially, at face value, and from our customary point of view. We do not like discussion, or talk, except for repartee; we are not much interested in the thought processes and minutely developed feelings of the characters; we tend to frown on all such

176

things as *not advancing the action*. Because we like rapidity of action, we like plays to have plots with a great many episodes; and we like plots with many lines of action, because these make for a great deal of suspense as well as unexpected developments. In the presence of Greek drama we are something like a certain contemporary journalist who watched a baseball game with a stop watch in his hand, and discovering that the ball was in actual play only some twenty minutes during two and a half hours, concluded that baseball was a very dull game. Baseball is not a dull game, and its excitement does not depend upon the time the ball is in play; it is a game of developing situations, and to understand and enjoy it you must be aware of these developing situations and the possibilities that may result from them. Chess is an even better example; your excitement depends not upon the speed of the moves but upon your full appreciation of the chess situation. To say this all once more: we like plots which are a great *aggregation* of incidents. That is our technique—*aggregation;* and we tend to think that our drama is the only drama, and that nothing else is dramatic.

But our drama is not the only drama, and aggregation is not the only dramatic technique. The technique opposite to aggregation is *isolation;* and it can be used quite as powerfully, with quite as much dramatic effect, as aggregation, provided we become aware of it and accustomed to it. The Oriental peoples seem always to have known the power of isolation; we Occidentals have seldom appreciated it. In *Gallions Reach* H. M. Tomlinson records the astonishment of an

Englishman on entering a room in a house in Penang and finding in it no article of furniture except a large vase on a stand; exquisite, it illumined and dominated the room, and afforded endless scope for contemplation. Where there are many things, none is likely to be contemplated; we respond at most to a harmony in their multiplicity. Where there is only one, we can contemplate.

I do not intend to imply that the technique of isolation, as I have called it, was a technique deliberately chosen by Aeschylus; rather, it was forced upon him by the condition of his art. Any art has its origin in the nature of man; that is, in elementary activities which are instinctive. In its first form it is apparently simply an *activity* enjoyable in itself, quite apart from the value of its product and practised by *anyone*. Thus children at play practise any art for which they have the means—music, sculpture, painting, dancing, and so on—and the fact that they do so in *play* shows that these activities are naturally pleasant. In a second stage, art develops in connection with some practical activity which it facilitates or renders more effective; work-songs grow out of various labors, and hymns and dirges grow out of the charms and prayers of religious or magical ceremonials. In this stage the practitioner of the art is naturally the practitioner of the occupation to which the art is subordinate. In a third stage, however, art develops in itself, beginning with the development of special skills in its practitioners and resulting in the creation of works which, independently of any practical end, have value in themselves. This is not to say that works of art produced in the earlier stages are artistically valueless, but that their possession of such value is incidental to some other end. The development of an art as an art is itself likely to involve three stages: materials must be provided; from some incidental combination of these there must result some effect which is recognized as valuable in its own right; and the materials must be re-worked and reorganized specifically to produce that effect.

So far as we know, Greek drama before Aeschylus had developed into a choric poem with some elements of drama, a form apparently brought to perfection by Phrynichus. It is Aeschylus who turned this form into drama itself. It will pay us to look a little more closely into the process by which Greek drama developed, for that process sheds much light on the nature of drama generally, and on the nature of specific forms as well. Drama, as I have said, is impossible without the impersonation of distinct dramatic entities. Homer himself did this, of course, in his epics, and passages in the Homeric epics testify that this was the practice of minstrels before him; but the device entered into the history of drama only when the *choragus,* or chorus leader, in the performance of the dithyramb, impersonated the god and indulged in a brief passage of dialog with the chorus. Thespis is said to have detached another member of the chorus to serve as "answerer"; dialog was now possible independently of the chorus. Moreover, Greek drama had evidently passed well beyond the phase of *monodrama,* in which different entities are impersonated by one actor. Phrynichus represented serious actions, dignified the verse and diction, and divided the chorus into separate bands, making

179

them in effect different dramatic entities. Even so, Greek drama remained predominantly choral in character; it was only with the introduction of a second actor by Aeschylus that a fairly extensive action could be depicted, and that dialog could become predominant. But the mere predominance of dialog does not necessarily bring about the existence of drama. So long as each speech is an end in itself, we are in the realm, not of drama, but of lyric or rhetoric. There is nothing dramatic about catechistic dialog, or dialectical dialog, for example; otherwise the Catechism or a Platonic dialog would be plays. Dialog becomes dramatic dialog strictly—that is, the kind of *dialog without which plays are impossible*—only when the speeches become verbal actions; when dialog, in other words, becomes interaction between the characters. It becomes so when it becomes subordinate to character and when character in turn becomes subordinate to action or plot. This construction of truly dramatic dialog, with the various alterations implied in it, is apparently the work of Aeschylus himself.

The dramatic form he devised still had its choral elements, and action still had consequently to be relatively brief. It was for Sophocles to contrive the more extended action, with a succession of episodes, which we have called a grand plot. Aeschylus used this and other Sophoclean innovations, but it is significant that in the *Oresteia,* at the end of his career, he deliberately reverts to the brief form of action. The *Oresteia* consists of three episodes—three short sequences of incidents centering about a principal event. The power of these episodes depends, not upon an elaborate dramatic context in which they are set, but upon their being separate, discrete, charged with the utmost force in themselves. In a word, isolation, as opposed to aggregation, and this brings us back to our point of beginning. What is the technique of isolation, and how does it work?

Far back in our discussion we saw that the proper size of an incident was that which included all the factors or causes requisite to give it probability and the proper kind and degree of emotional power, as determined by the function of the incident. We saw, too, that the size of an incident ranged from the general and simple idea of it to extremely complex ideas, developed in their circumstantial components, in the greatest possible detail. Now, when an incident is part of a system of incidents, it is governed by the system of which it is a part and cannot be fully and completely developed in itself. It must be curtailed or extended or otherwise shaped by the pressure of its context. Just as there is a difference between a lyric, which is a whole in itself, and which can be fully rounded and developed to make it as effective as possible, and the dramatic speech, which is not a whole and cannot be developed as if it were one, there is a difference between the incident which stands alone and one which must be determined by its position in a particular sequence.

The action of the *Agamemnon* is one *single* deed—the murder of the king. This may sound a little odd; any child can see that a succession of incidents is exhibited on the stage. But there is a very great difference between such a succession as we have here, and such a succession as we find in *Hamlet* or *Macbeth*. The Shakespearian action contains many essential and factorial incidents, and cannot be adequately summarized in terms of a single incident, however central. Such an action as we have in the *Agamemnon,* however, may be summarized thus: all the incidents surrounding the central incident of the murder are merely dramatized *circumstances* of that murder. There is one essential incident; there are a few factorial incidents; all others are incidents of representation. Or, to put this a little differently, Aeschylus' dramatic method is analytic, as opposed to Shakespeare's synthetic method. Shakespeare builds a system of essential incidents; Aeschylus takes a single essential incident and analyzes it into its circumstantial components.

But, you may say, you are treating the *Agamemnon* as if it were not part of a trilogy. The *trilogy* certainly offers a succession of essential incidents. That is certainly true, but there is a difference between a succession of three complete *wholes* and a succession of *parts*. The three plays of the *Oresteia* are complete plays; the Acts which make up a Shakespearian tragedy are not.

If the action of the *Agamemnon* is a single deed analyzed into its circumstances, how are those circumstances contrived to give it its force? The deed itself is what Aristotle calls the *tragic deed;* and the tragic deed, in his sense, is some act destructive either of the life or the happiness of the victim, and an act committed, not by a stranger or an enemy, but by someone who should have been friendly to him. It is a deed which arouses pity and fear, and we can piece out the

182

sparse discussion of it in the *Poetics* with remarks that Aristotle makes about these emotions in the *Rhetoric*. Our pity is greatest when the victim is noble; when, after long privation and suffering, he has finally triumphed, and is cut off before he can enjoy his triumph; when the disaster strikes at the moment when he thinks himself most secure, prosperous, loved, and otherwise happy; when disaster comes from an unexpected source, as from a hand that should have been friendly; when it occurs in circumstances in which it might easily have been prevented, say, with help readily at hand, and when there were warnings of it which with a little luck he might have heeded; when the disaster is undeserved. It is scarcely necessary to observe that Aeschylus has worked all this into the death of Agamemnon. Professor Kitto remarks in his *Greek Tragedy* that Aristotle has nothing to do with Aeschylus. I wonder.

Aeschylus' ultimate intention, however, is not to arouse pity for Agamemnon. When in the ignorance of my youth I objected because Agamemnon does not speak until line 810 of a play not quite 1700 lines long, I was going on the assumption that a play is always named after its chief character or protagonist. A false assumption: the libation-bearers and the Furies are not the protagonists of the succeeding plays, either. The *Agamemnon* is Clytemnestra's play; the king is merely the victim. It is not so much the matter of his *dying* as of her *killing* that engrosses us.

The tragic deed is hers, not his; and what is especially tragic about it is that it is a horrible deed, done deliberately with full knowledge of its character as an act, in all respects but one; and yet, because of that one respect, it is in the end done in ignorance and mistakenly. For she knows everything about the act except its consequences.

She kills the king for a number of motives. Some of these may seem base. For example, one of these is certainly the desire to protect herself and her paramour, and to secure the reign. But she is also obtaining justice for the killing of Iphigenia; and, what is more important still, she fancies that by killing him she will put an end to the curse upon the house of Atreus, that by her bloody act she will put an end to bloodshed, cleanse the house of its contamination, and establish justice. This last motive cannot be doubted; she declares it to the Chorus when she has completely exposed herself, and she mentions it to Aegisthus as a thing known, indeed resolved upon, by both of them. Her last lines are "You and I, henceforward, shall govern all things well." She does a dreadful thing, to establish justice; and our pity is evoked for Agamemnon, and for Cassandra, too, primarily to make us feel the dreadfulness of it.

But indeed we can hardly understand what these motives mean, apart from the woman herself. She is undoubtedly a bad woman, a wicked woman; but it is impossible not to respect her, not to admire her. She is a woman of profound passions: her hatred for Agamemnon is so intense and so deep that she thirsts for his death, and she says that when she felt herself spattered with his blood she rejoiced as the corn when it receives the rain. Fierce as her passions are, she has them under absolute control; she is calm and resolute, and so much mistress of every situation that she is

able to sport with her interlocutors, in language filled
with ironies and ambiguities. She is both cautious and
daring. She is a woman really unique, not to be described in general attributes; one must look at the
particulars of her actions to see her; and even when
one has studied these, she remains a being profoundly
mysterious.

Her principal wile is her femininity. She insists upon
that again and again, knowing that as long as she em-
phasizes that, no one will suspect her, for no one as-
sociates a character like hers, or such deeds as she con-
templates, with womanhood. In reality she is "mascu-
line-minded," not feminine. There is very great irony
in that the watchman, the Chorus, and others faintly
and dimly recognize this in her, without in the least
understanding the full implications of this. The watchman speaks of her *androboulon elpidon,* her man-
minded confidence. The Chorus at line 351 says to her
Gunai, kat'andra sophron euphronos legeis, Woman,
you speak with the prudence of a prudent man. And
there is further irony in the fact that the Chorus comes
to distrust her report *because she is a woman,* and because women are gullible.

We have to grasp something of how much the seriousness of the play depends upon the poet's contrivance
of his characters. The action is tragic, not because
Agamemnon is a king and Clytemnestra a queen, but
because both are *conceived as regal*—which is a very
different thing. Every word that Clytemnestra speaks
is pregnant with pride, imperiousness, majesty. The
pride is apparent even when she speaks with apparent
humility. The king too is royal, brief as his role is;

and the crime is more appalling because a woman of such dignity commits it upon a man of such dignity. Take from Agamemnon his loftiness, his confidence, his forthrightness; make him mean, timid, suspicious, cunning; and at once his murder becomes a crime merely sordid. Take from Clytemnestra her resolute calm, her masculine fortitude, her mysterious and passionate nature; make her irresolute, timorous, appalled by the deed she must do, unable to disguise her feelings and intentions; and again we no longer have the same seriousness of action.

Yet that seriousness is due to the contrivance of the action itself, also, in its particular circumstances. It will be useful to compare Aeschylus' dramatic version with that of another great poet. Homer gives, in fact, two principal accounts, Proteus' tale in Book IV, and Agamemnon's own in Book XI of the *Odyssey*. It is impossible to say whether Aeschylus founded directly upon these or used other accounts, and it is perfectly irrelevant in any case. The question is how the *Agamemnon* is contrived and what is good or bad about such contrivance, not what it founds upon.

Here is Proteus' tale:

Now there was a watchman whom Aegisthus kept always on the watch and to whom he had promised two talents of gold. The man had been looking out for a whole year to make sure that Agamemnon did not give him the slip and prepare war; when therefore the man saw Agamemnon go by, he went and told Aegisthus who at once began to lay a plot for him. He picked twenty of his bravest warriors and placed them in an ambuscade on one side of the cloister while on the opposite side he prepared a banquet. Then he sent his chariots and horsemen to Agamemnon and invited him to the feast, but he meant foul play. He got him there all unsuspicious of the doom that was awaiting him and killed him when the banquet was over as though he were butchering an ox in the shambles; not one of Agamemnon's followers was left alive nor yet one of Aegisthus, but they were all killed there in the cloisters.

Agamemnon's own story is in general agreement with this, except that he attributes the plot to "Aegisthus and my wicked wife," and says "I heard Priam's daughter Cassandra scream as Clytemnestra killed her close beside me."

Simply let us ask a few questions here. Would it have been better to leave Clytemnestra out, as Proteus does, and have Aegisthus the only plotter and murderer? No; the tragic quality would have been lost. We should simply have enemy murdering enemy, and the only element of horror would have been in the sufferings of the victim or the brutality of the killing. Would it have been better to have Agamemnon somewhat advised of what was going on, so that he might possibly prepare war? No; we should then simply have cunning against cunning, and the character of Agamemnon would have been lowered. How about the banquet? Is that better? And apparently there is some time-lapse after the war; what of that? And shall we have a universal massacre? And shall we leave Cassandra out? Or is it more tragic that Agamemnon should come home, at the height of his triumph, to be greeted by an adoring city and an apparently faithful wife, to have his way paved with such luxury and splendor that he fears to tread upon it, to have him persuaded to tread it

187

precisely in deference to his faithful and adoring wife, and to have that very way lead him to his death?

We might carry this farther; but I think it is perfectly unnecessary. You may find out anything you wish to know further simply by asking what happens to the action if you leave something out, and put something in, or alter something.

The seriousness of the action does not derive simply from the fact that it involves individuals of worth. It comes out of great and prolonged calamities and is to eventuate in more. It involves a noble family, generations of it. It involves the happiness of a nation. It involves a principle of justice upon which man's conduct must depend if he is to be man and not beast. Aeschylus everywhere gives us the sense of these prodigious issues and consequences. And he gives us, too, the sense of the terrible blindness of mankind, even when they suppose they see. Clytemnestra with her calm confidence in her knowledge of herself, Orestes with the counsel of a god in his ear, are still blind as Oedipus. They do not foresee, they do not know what they do. Man as an individual cannot know justice and cannot pursue it; for men and for gods there must be law.

So far we have been talking about the general contrivance of the action of the play. We must now consider the representation. As I said much earlier, while the plot determines the general reactions of the audience, the representation determines specifically what emotions are felt, in what degree, and in what order; for it determines what is known to the audience at any given point, and knowledge is the principal cause of emotion.

We may observe first of all what may be called the general representational strategy of the play. A great deal of the effect of the representation depends on keeping the character of Clytemnestra a mystery, an enigma. We are kept in suspense by the discrepancy between what she seems and what we suspect, and the ultimate revelation of her character comes suddenly and unexpectedly. Almost all other parts of the representation consist of dramatizings of the circumstances which, as we saw earlier, give the deed its tragic power.

Let us see, in part at least, how this works particularly. What ought to be shown upon the stage? If the character of Clytemnestra must be kept enigmatic, if the fundamental suspense and surprise as well as the tragic emotions depend upon the character of the murder as a moral act, the audience must not be allowed to know much more—if anything—than the Chorus. The poet must avoid exhibiting any scene which would give us too significant a clue to her character. Thus the actual announcement to her of the fall of Troy cannot be shown, for in such a scene she must either reveal her true feelings and purposes, or not. If she does, the enigma is at an end; if she does not, the scene will lack excitement entirely, or depend for excitement simply on the news of the victory. (There is the additional difficulty, of course, that this would have somehow to be done in the presence of the Chorus.) It is better to concentrate on the news itself, at its origin; thus we have the watchman scene.

In the scene in which Clytemnestra first enters, we see her announcing the news to the Chorus of Elders, and they disbelieve her. Why must we have this scene? Long ago we saw that if an action is probable only as happening under special circumstances, it must be shown on stage as happening in those circumstances; we found this one reason, at least, why Shakespeare had to represent Mark Antony actually persuading the Roman populace. It is a general improbability that a single speech should reverse the public mind; it is similarly a general improbability that Clytemnestra should be able to deceive all about her. Hence Aeschylus has to show her in very fact deceiving the Elders, together with the wiles by which she does so. Chief among these, as I said, is her femininity, and we see its effect in that she is disbelieved when she is speaking the truth. (Agamemnon is indeed led to his death by it.) And in this expository scene we are shown all the traits which imply what she is and what she will do, without our being able to draw the startling but obvious inference.

The scene with the herald prepares for the return of Agamemnon. In this scene, too, Clytemnestra is proved right; and the Chorus acknowledges this, without seeing the full implications of it. Had they penetrated her mask, Agamemnon might have been saved. And this scene is one of several points in the action at which the catastrophe might have been averted. These resemble the warnings which Caesar disregards in Shakespeare, and I think they are rather more subtle. But they have the same effect. Two lines of action make up the plot of the tragedy—the line of the co-plotters and the line of those who may intervene. The latter threatens repeatedly to converge with the former, but never does. There is no complication, only threatened complication.

Agamemnon's scene exhibits another threatened convergence. If Clytemnestra has gone too far in her blandishments, if Agamemnon suspects, even if he merely becomes displeased, the whole plan may collapse. And the plan threatens again to collapse when Agamemnon has entered the palace, and Cassandra does not follow him, despite the commands and imprecations of Clytemnestra. She remains silent—a deliberate reversion on the poet's part to the older technique of having one person remain mute while two speakers discourse —but what an employment of a mute! What a silence, in answer to Clytemnestra's desperate attempts to induce her to go in! A significant, a portentous, a terrible silence—the most dreadful silence in all drama. Clytemnestra herself, in her all but unshakable calm, is shaken by that silence: for the first time her mask falls; she discloses something of the proud, arrogant woman she is; she withdraws.

And then we have, once she is gone, Cassandra's sudden, wild, and mysterious outburst. *Alas, alas,* she cries; mysteriously she calls upon Apollo; cryptically she recalls his name as the way-god, who has led her into this way of death. Notice the misconstructions of the Chorus as she recounts the horrors of the past, the present, and the time to be, and the bitter ironies of these; the succession of wild emotions she exhibits, the strange effects of these upon the Chorus; till she weakens, becomes resigned, enters the house of death, the Chorus still uncomprehending; and then, at last, there comes the death-cry of Agamemnon.

It would seem impossible to exceed the dramatic force of these scenes; but Clytemnestra's ultimate revelation to the Chorus of her true character and of the crime itself does exceed it. I think that any audience, hearing her fearful joy in her crime, must be as stunned as the Chorus itself. And this astonishment continues to the very last line, which reveals the ultimate motive. It is her speech to Aegisthus which I have quoted before: "Henceforward you and I shall govern all things well."

Powerful as this play is, its construction is one of extremest simplicity: a two-line action, with threatened convergences which fail to complicate; a representation which shows the points of threatened convergence, dramatizes the circumstances of the tragic deed, and, after gradually revealing the character of the protagonist, suddenly makes an overwhelming revelation.

A word about the Chorus. Aeschylus not merely employs it as a group of real persons in the drama but as a very important group. The Argive Elders do not simply stand about and comment. They are a force, a power in the play that must be dealt with. Old as they are, they can prevent the murder of the king, if once they suspect; Clytemnestra herself knows that and deals most carefully with them. And they have other dramatic purposes: although they do not know, until too late, the particular event in which they are participating, they are always aware, they make *us* constantly aware, of the greater tragedy that lies behind the tragedy of Agamemnon; of the massive web of crime, horror, suffering, and shame of which his murder is merely a detail.

The dramatic mastery of Aeschylus becomes the more obvious if we compare his play with the *Agamemnon* of Seneca. In the Roman work, the action is converted simply into a set of occasions for set speeches. Character is limited to the kind of impersonation that was used in the exercise and contests of the rhetorical schools. It is not character realized in verbal action but character as a formula or convention governing what can be said. Dialog takes a precedence over action, and it is not what I have called dramatic dialog, but catechistic, dialectical, or rhetorical. The Chorus is used only nominally as a person of the drama. It is uninvolved in the action, it comments only, and its comments are unconnected with the play, or so general as to have little reference to it. Far from seeing greater significance in the action than the immediate participants or the audience, it fails to see even what is obvious.

The action, in itself not a dramatic one in construction, loses all dramatic immediacy. Moreover, every chance for suspense is foregone: the character of Clytemnestra is fully revealed to us, together with her plans, in her very first speech; and so with everything else. Since all force of action is lost, the dramatist has to fall back upon the resources of language alone; that is, he relies upon poetic imagery or metaphor to do for him what the action itself should have done primarily.

Every decadence of drama involves a reliance upon devices and materials which are not essentially dramatic. Greek tragedy arose out of non-dramatic materials; Roman tragedy was a reversion to those materials.

VIII
King Lear

King Lear is an extraordinary work. The world has looked at it, called it extraordinary, even superhuman —and proceeded to find fault with it. For some unaccountable reason the play makes people want to tinker with it. There are marked differences between the quarto of 1608 and the so-called "bad quarto" which, though it brazenly bears the same date, was published two years later; and there are marked differences between both quartos and the Folio of 1623; and I suspect that the chief reason for these differences is tinkering. Bibliographers may disagree with me, but if they do they may force me to confess that sometimes I suspect them of tinkering too. Actors and playwrights have tinkered very briskly with King Lear. Nahum Tate made a version of it, produced in 1681, which in his opinion improved it vastly: he changed the ending to a happy one, kicked out the Fool, and built in a love story—a love "betwixt Edgar and Cordelia," he says, "that never changed word with each other in the original." Obviously he feels this was immensely clever tinkering and the world seems to have thought so too, for a while, for this version had no rival until Garrick's version of 1756. Garrick tinkered, too, with this advantage, that he could tinker both with Shakespeare and with Tate. In 1768 Colman tinkered the great love of Edgar and Cordelia out of the play; but he admired Tate's master stroke of the happy ending so much that he tinkered the rest of the play to fit it. In 1809 Kemble tinkered back into the play some tinkerings of Tate that Garrick had tinkered out. The happy ending lasted throughout the eighteenth century— lasted, in fact, until Kean put *that* matter right in 1823. The Fool did not get back into the play until Macready restored him, along with everything else, in 1838.

While all this was going on the critics were extremely critical; for a critic, like Iago, is "nothing if not critical." But the fact is they also wanted to tinker. Samuel Johnson objected to the description of Dover Cliff. Goethe objected to the first scene. Johnson and Coleridge objected to the blinding of Gloucester. So did Joseph Warton, who also objected to the sub-plot as a whole, and thought that perhaps Goneril and Regan were a little bit *too* bad. Lamb liked the poetry, thought it was a great *reading* play, but said flatly "the Lear of Shakespeare cannot be acted." And so on. I say "And so on," because this chapter is not a history of tinkering, though it is beginning to sound as if it were, and because the tinkering is still going on. Olivier's version of King Lear, for example, changed Lear into a whimsical sort of elf, as Wilson Knight complains; and for that matter, Wilson Knight has done a little tinkering on his own.

Amid all this tinkering, certain questions recur and recur. Why does Lear devise that "silly trick," as Coleridge calls it, of demanding that the daughters profess their love? Why does Cordelia refuse? Why is the plot so complicated? Why are there so many characters? Why the parallel story of Gloucester? Why must Gloucester's eyes be put out on stage? Why should Lear and Cordelia die?

G. B. Harrison has said that Shakespearian study as a whole may be classified according to three points of view: the point of view of the scholar, that of the literary critic, and that of the actor and producer. Quite so, I say, and I note that one point of view is conspicuously missing. It is rather a nice point of view, and I suspect it is somewhat more like Shakespeare's own than any of the others. It is the point of view of the *working dramatist*. I wish to take it for a while. I have a feeling that it may settle many of these questions.

Things look quite different from this point of view, much as they do back-stage. A work of art is always a collocation of artificial causes which produce natural effects: the scholar, the critic, the actor, the producer, and the public see everything in terms of the effects; the artist has to operate among the causes which produce those effects; so you see, they are quite at different ends of the stick. Let me warn you about one thing, though; I am not going to let you into the inner secret workings of Shakespeare's mind. These are things perfectly individual with Shakespeare, and how one gets at them I have no idea. But the *art of the drama* is not individual with Shakespeare; the *art of tragedy* is the same for Shakespeare and for the worst playwright who ever lived, just as the art of playing the piano is the same art, whether one is a Horowitz or a beginner. The same technical problems exist and the same possible methods of their solution. All that we shall see is a dramatist who has one general problem which involves a whole complex of special problems and who tries, like any other artist, to solve them in the best possible way.

The general problem is this, that he wants to make a tragedy based on the old Lear materials. The Lear story is quite a familiar one; Geoffrey of Monmouth, Wace, Layamon, Robert of Gloucester, Robert Manning, John Harding, Robert Fabyan, and John Rastell, among others, had all handled it; two versions of it had come down in the *Gesta Romanorum;* and there are even a good many Elizabethan versions, among them the one in Holinshed's *Chronicles,* that in Spenser's *The Faery Queene,* that in *The Mirror for Magistrates,* and even an earlier anonymous play; and these last are probably known to our dramatist. It does not really matter, however, for our present purposes; and we need not worry about the differences between the different versions. The general outline of the story is the same: a king asks his daughters how much they love him; the false daughters make satisfactory answers, the true one does not; the annoyed king banishes her, and sooner or later afterward either gives away his kingdom or is despoiled of it; rejected by the false daughters, he undergoes various troubles; and finally, through the kind offices of the youngest and faithful daughter, gets his kingdom back again.

It is a simple little yarn, with the moral sticking out a mile. Originally, perhaps, it was some sort of moral apolog which became a folk tale, was dignified into history by the chroniclers, and was humanized somewhat by the poets. On the whole, not too promising, one would say; but our dramatist wants to make a tragedy of it. I am sure that any self-respecting critic would have advised him against the project, though Cleanth Brooks might have said that it would pass if he put in a paradox or two, and William Empson might have said it would work if only he were ambiguous enough. Such a humble little sow's ear, to be made into a silk purse! But it is the artist's business to make such sow's ears into silk purses, and this artist is Shakespeare.

Even so, he has his problems. To begin with, the tale, in its anecdotal form at least, is not tragic, not even particularly moving; it is about a piece of silliness and is itself rather silly. It is merely an illustration of the old saw that actions speak louder than words, and it appeals only to the faculty of moral judgment; you can only nod gravely at stories of that sort and start a new conversation as quickly as possible, for it leads to nothing. That is—unless you happen to see something more in it. In the basic tale the king is a mere abstraction, a generality, a counter; what if one replaced that abstraction with a real person? And the kind of person, here, makes all the difference; Shakespeare knew from his own experience that the same basic tale can be funny in the Pyramus and Thisbe of *A Midsummer Night's Dream,* and tragic in *Romeo and Juliet,* according as the same things happen to different people and in different circumstances. For —although the *events* remain the same—the *acts* differ as they are performed by different people for different motives; and their fortunes differ also, as deserved or undeserved, important or unimportant to the characters involved; consequently their emotional effect on us must differ as well.

If the play is to be made tragic, what must the character of Lear be made to be? In the first place, if we are to feel any great pity for him, his misfortunes must be undeserved, which means that he must have elements of nobility in him. But he cannot be a perfect man; as Socrates remarks, the perfectly good man cannot be used as a tragic figure (an error that Addison made in his *Cato*, by the way); the perfect man cannot be humbled, he will not weep or lament, he is as safe as man can be, and even in his misfortunes we admire rather than pity him. Moreover, the act which Lear performs—that of deliberately banishing and disinheriting a loving daughter—is a peculiar one. If it is done deliberately and with full knowledge, it is a base and cold-hearted act. If it is done through sheer stupidity or whim or pettiness, it is regrettable, contemptible, perhaps ridiculous, but it is not tragic. To be made tragic, it must stem from compulsion or passion or incomplete knowledge; and though it is not a right action, it must *seem* right action—that is, it cannot be a piece of *knowing* injustice—to Lear at the time he commits it. Again, if it stems from some passion—anger, for instance—that anger will have to be of the right kind. No one is good or bad simply because he is angry; but different moral characters exhibit the same passion differently and under different circumstances: the petty man exhibits anger in a petty way and for causes which are important only to the petty, whereas the nobler man is indignant in a nobler way and for causes which are important only to the nobler. If Lear is to be angry, it must be with royal anger, such anger as befits a king, and for such cause as befits a king.

Let us examine the whole action. Critics have criticized everything about it; the irrational folly of dividing the kingdom, of demanding the profession of love, of disinheriting Cordelia; and it seems to me that not all of their objections are well taken. Why does Lear divide the kingdom? Because he is without male issue; consequently he has no real successor; consequently he wishes to avert war between the pretenders after his death by an equal division. Why does he abrogate authority? Because he is becoming too old to rule, and because he thinks that if the division is made in his lifetime and established as a going concern, there is less chance of war. And what is the point of his demanding the public profession of love? Well, in *part* it is this: if Lear is giving up his authority and still wants security and dignity, he can only trust to their *love;* and his insistence upon their public profession of it is an attempt to have it warranted and witnessed as a formal part of the compact of the delivery of property and power.

I say "in part" for there is more to it than that, but before I can explain I must digress a little. In Greek tragedy, while the tragic situation is usually brought about by the decrees of the Fates or by the intervention of gods in human affairs, as in the *Hippolytus,* or by a curse, as in the *Oresteia,* the tragic character *does* something that renders him especially liable and vulnerable to it. Roman tragedy, if Seneca is representative, is simply fatalistic; the characters are the passive instruments for the accomplishment of fate. But Shakespeare has worked out his own formula for the tragic *hamartia,* the tragic mistake; and so far as I know, it is one peculiar to him. A little review of some of the major tragic figures will make it clear. What is Hamlet? A philosopher and scholar by training and temperament, a speculative thinker who is not concerned with action. In what situation must he act? In a practical one, in which speculation is bound to be disastrous. What is Othello? A general, and a general must take the advice of his most trusted lieutenants. Othello is put in a situation in which it is disastrous to do so. Coriolanus is also a general; now, a general does not *solicit* support, he commands it; Coriolanus is put in a situation where he must solicit it. Macbeth is a soldier who has elevated himself by conspicuous courage; it is through taunting him about his courage that his wife at last drives him to murder Duncan. In brief, the thing is this: a character of conspicuous virtues and abilities, who has distinguished himself through them in one sphere, is thrown suddenly into a sphere of action in which to exercise them—and he *must* exercise them—is to invoke catastrophe. A far sadder notion than the Greek: we fall, not through our vices merely, but even through our virtues. The *hamartia,* the tragic error, is still there; but it has been transmuted into a mistake rendered inevitable by all that the character has been and has done. Disaster comes, not through the fates or the gods, but by human agency alone. In Lear's case, Lear is a feudal lord; he is thrown into a domestic sphere where the laws of feudality do not operate, for he is abrogating the authority on which feudality depends.

This strange act of his, then, *as Shakespeare constructs it,* is nothing other than that of a feudal lord demanding the profession of fealty from his vassals, as a condition of the conveyance of authority and property. He gives in this feudal way and he demands in this feudal way, for it is the only way he knows. He is still remaining king; he retains for himself "the name and all the additions to a king," not realizing that without army, kingdom, or authority, no king can be king. Look at these strangely formal speeches, with their legal phrasing, and everything becomes clear. After Goneril's answer, Lear responds:

> Of all these bounds, even from this line to this,
> With shadowy forests and with champains rich'd
> With plenteous rivers and wide-skirted meads,
> We make thee lady: to thine and Albany's issue
> Be this perpetual.

After Regan's answer, Lear says:

> To thee and thine hereditary ever
> Remain this ample third of our fair kingdom;
> No less in space, validity, and pleasure
> Than that conferred on Goneril.

These are the speeches of a feudal lord, to vassals who have professed fealty. Thus Shakespeare has solved one part of the problem; if now Lear is wrong, and of course he is, he at least is wrong on principle, and a kingly principle. Cordelia's famous obstinacy comes from her complete inability to understand the feudal character of Lear's action, as his own unfatherly response to her comes from the fact that here he is not acting as a father at all; he is acting in the role of lord to vassal. In his view it is particularly wounding that she, his favorite, should refuse to participate in what are to him necessary formalities, and her refusal casts doubt on her whole relation to him. How *can* she, in his view, be a loving daughter, when she refuses to take part in the only pact that hereafter can assure his continuing status as *king?* In *Julius Caesar,* Brutus comes to grief by imposing the ethical upon the political; Lear comes to grief by imposing the feudal upon the familial.

For the familial and the feudal do not mix. They are like countries with contrary laws, so that an act which is lawful in the one is criminal in the other. The one demands forms and contracts; the other depends wholly upon trust. A feudal lord may demand the exclusive loyalty of his vassal; a father can make no such demand upon his daughter's affection. The nature of love and affection is that they are inexhaustible, that consequently they cannot be limited to any one object. Hence any profession to that effect is by that very fact a *lie.* Cordelia knows this, and cannot make it. Lear does not; moreover, in demanding of love that it be secured to himself alone, he is committing an act, not of love, but of selfishness which is the contrary of love. Lear is ignorant of the nature of love; he must be taught it. He begins in selfishness, thinking of himself; let him end, himself forgotten, wholly absorbed in the beloved.

We have something of the character of Lear, now, for we know he must be the kind of man capable of an act such as I have described and for the reasons described; but he must also be capable of the tragic suffering and of what we may call, for the moment, the tragic resolution. I say "the" suffering and "the" resolution to imply both that these must be of a certain general kind and that these must be appropriate to *him* as a character. What shape must his sufferings take? He has sinned against love, demanded from it what it cannot give, what should not be demanded of it; his sufferings must be the atonement for this; he must discover the meaning of love through the privation of love. Without love and benevolence and the humane feelings, man becomes a beast, justice and law become empty forms, authority becomes mere force, and the world becomes the nightmare of cannibalistic nature where all prey on all. Lear has driven love away for the sake of empty forms; he must fall into that nightmare world and suffer in it.

But suffer how? In John Higgins' narrative in *The Mirror for Magistrates,* Lear's sons-in-law revolt and seize power (the profession of love here has nothing to do with the division of the kingdom, but only with Cordelia's banishment), after which Lear's retinue is steadily reduced as he goes from daughter to daughter. Spenser says of the daughters simply that they "his cheare empayrd." Perhaps that can be kept; but it must be dignified, for our Lear cannot be seen simply as an old man in petty rage because, so to speak, his allowance has been cut. It can be dignified if a nobler issue can be involved in it; then its very triviality in turn ennobles it, for your man of nobility will be apt "greatly to find quarrel in a straw when honor's at the stake."

We must see Lear, then, in deteriorating fortunes; but his sufferings cannot come from these in themselves; they must come from a higher principle involved. Shall the daughters inflict bodily harm upon him? No; actual physical pain would indeed *detract* from his sufferings; they must be wholly mental even though they are experienced in circumstances of physical privation. Moreover, the harm or injury from the daughters must be kept as slight as possible; it must be the great principle involved which gives the offense its tragic magnitude. This alone must torment Lear; the point must even be emphasized that, whatever privation he may endure, he is insensible to it in comparison; it is no part of the real cause. Here we have, of course, the genesis of the storm scenes, and one of the themes of Lear's speeches during them.

Thus the main elements of the plot begin to take form: Lear must endure degradation from kingship, and to suffer from this *on principle,* i.e., as an affront to his *honor,* he must be proud; he must suffer ingratitude and betrayal, and to suffer from these *on principle* he must be just; he must suffer from the privation of affection, and to suffer from this as deeply as possible he must be the kind of man to whom affection is most necessary, and to whom affection may well outweigh all other things. Each of Shakespeare's great tragic heroes pays in his own personal coin, the kind that costs him most: the courageous Macbeth in moral terror, the intellectual Hamlet in doubt and confusion;

and the proud, just, affectionate Lear must pay in the suffering of humiliation, injustice, and the privation of affection. What shall mark the extremity of his torment? Madness: he sees the world he has chosen and it maddens him. So Shakespeare's Lear is the only Lear to go mad, for he is the only Lear so fashioned that he is capable of the ultimate mental torment. To be profoundly shaken we must be profoundly made.

He is also the only Lear to come to an unhappy end; the Lears of the other versions have their kingdoms restored, and die of old age. Why must we have *this* ending? Is it made necessary or probable by the antecedent action? It is not. As a matter of fact the catastrophe *seldom* is in the great tragedies of Shakespeare. What in the plot necessitates that Emilia should come too late to save Desdemona? Hamlet's death-wound, poisoned though the sword is, is a mere possibility of combat. The defeat of Cordelia's forces is the mere fortune of war, and nothing prevents Edmund from speaking in time to save Cordelia. The catastrophe is no more probable than its contrary; and yet we must have the unhappy ending. Why? Because it is an *emotional* necessity.

But again we may ask: *why?* Because the bullfight is incomplete without death? Because tragedy, as some have thought, is basically ritualistic and hence sacrifice is demanded? Because, as Charles Lamb thought, our sympathies have otherwise been engaged in vain? None of these answers seems to me satisfactory. This is no point at which to embark on the poetics of tragedy; let me simply say that in every true tragedy the audience is compelled to transcend a *lower* set of moral values to a *higher;* it is compelled to fear and pity, for instance, only to acknowledge in the end that in a higher judgment there are worse evils than those it has been fearing and pitying; and by confronting great misery it has learned, momentarily at least, something of the great conditions upon which human happiness truly depends, and something of the high dignity of which man is capable. This, of course, is precisely the tragic *catharsis* of which Aristotle spoke. Frequently in tragedy—in *Lear,* for instance—the tragic hero himself experiences that transcendence of values, and his merest acknowledgment of that experience is in itself a human triumph. Lear must forget royal pride and the stings of ingratitude and all else, and realize the supreme value of love; he must put by his kingship and all the world, gladly, for the sake of his loved daughter; and then he must learn the value of love again as only loss can teach it; and so Cordelia must die. Her effort to save Lear, then, must be in vain; her death may follow naturally on her defeat; otherwise it will be difficult to bring about.

And so must Lear die. Ingratitude could only drive him to madness; love brings his death. He may be given this mercy, at least, that he dies fancying that Cordelia is reviving.

We have now seen how the main line of the action had to be developed and how the character of Lear had to be framed. What of Cordelia? She need hardly appear; she exists simply so that Lear may love and reject and love again. Her character is very simple; she needs only to be made the perfect daughter. (By the way, I think it is incorrect to call her "obstinate,"

208

as critics have done; she is only *persistently candid,* and
deep affection *is* candid; those critics who have supposed her obstinate because she does not accede to
Lear's demands have failed to understand her integ-
rity.)

What of Goneril and Regan? Higgins calls them
"vipers" and "devilish beasts"; but all they do in *his*
tale is to treat Lear quite well for a while, and then cut
his retinue. Why *must* they, in this play, be made real
vipers, beasts, devils? George Bernard Shaw has criticized Shakespeare's villains as melodramatic and untrue; but in this instance at least he has not realized
that Shakespeare is dealing with a higher truth than
his own. Man, ruled absolutely by self-interest, perfectly deprived of any benevolent concern for others,
can *only* be evil; and he will *do* evil in any degree that
his self-interest demands. Goneril and Regan *must* be
evil then, but evil in a special way; they do not do evil
for its own sake, they do it for their own. They are not
even cruel, for instance, for they do not *enjoy* the infliction of pain; but they will commit any cruelty in
order to achieve their ends, or out of rage that their
aims have been thwarted. Indeed, they do not enjoy
anything; they are the most joyless creatures in Shakespeare; no contentment is possible to them, for they
are always bent upon a further aim.

We must show what these villains are really capable
of, in *deeds;* at the same time, as we saw earlier, they
cannot visit their full cruelty on Lear, for he must be
wholly rapt in his own mental anguish. Hence we must
have another victim in the play (here enters Gloucester), to be cruelly used by them, for far less reason; for

that will show what they are ultimately capable of doing to Lear himself. We must see them progress ever deeper into evil, as their self-interests demand; they must move from lies to trivial treachery to trivial conspiracy to filial neglect to actual conspiracy against their father's life, to sister-murder and self-murder at last; for in their nightmare world, thus the dark stair of self descends, and ends. Lear never has knowledge of the full evil of their *actions;* he surmises what *they* are, as *beings,* from relatively small things, and that is enough.

The main line of the action, even as we have developed it with the addition of these characters, still presents grave dramatic problems. First, Lear's tragic deed—this is of course his foolish banishment of Cordelia—is the *initiating action* of the plot, as opposed to Othello's which occurs almost at the end; thus the plot can only be the history of its consequences to the final catastrophe. Moreover, Lear's act is a peculiar one, for it renders him powerless as an agent. Hamlet, Macbeth, Coriolanus, Othello, all can *do* something in the action. Lear cannot. He can only suffer; all effective action is up to others. Can he at least, as he does both in Higgins' and Spenser's versions, go to Cordelia and ask for aid? He cannot. He will lose all tragic stature, his sufferings are self-imposed, if it is possible for him to go to her at any time. What is to prevent him from going to her? Primarily, the fact *that* he *thinks* it impossible; how should Cordelia, whom he had disinherited and banished, love him when her sisters, whom he had benefited, did not? No, he can do nothing. Consequently, there must be some agent who can act in his behalf, at least to bring his plight to Cordelia's attention, or some force to bring Lear and Cordelia together again.

Again—if Cordelia is defeated and dies, and we have seen that she must—what is to happen to Goncril and Regan? Since they live in the world of *self*, there must be, at the very least, some object in which their interests are opposed. Also, as we saw, there must be another victim besides Lear, to exhibit to the full the evil capacities of Goneril and Regan. But more important than any is this difficulty—that even if the plot is to involve the greater and greater sufferings of Lear, and the greater and greater dangers to Lear, the action will *steadily lose power*. An audience will not endure an unbroken and extended tale of misfortune; human nature cannot remain for very long in the same emotion, it is too inconstant. There are limits to pity and fear: the audience without hope for the future of Lear will become bored and indifferent, and the effect will be dreary and lugubrious rather than tragic. Consequently there must be some action, at least to interrupt the Lear line; better still, to *reinforce* it; to raise false hopes for him again and again; for when the audience has been led to hope for the tragic figure, and that hope is frustrated, it feels more forcibly than ever the agony of his plight.

Now the main line cannot be developed to take care of all these matters; consequently there is only one solution: there must be a *sub-plot*. The moment we conceive the necessity of it, certain things are clear at once. It must turn on the same issues, it must belong to the same moral world, or it will weaken the main line; for the audience will feel that, however bad Lear's case, it is, so to speak, only a local, not a universal matter. If the sub-plot is to contain an agent of retribution, that agent must be prevented from effective action until the end (this will develop into Edgar and Edgar's hunted condition). If it is to contain an object of contention between Goneril and Regan, what shall that be, a kingdom, a treasure, or a man? (Thus we have Edmund.) Moreover, the sub-plot though it must be pathetic must not be tragic; that is, though the events must be sad, they must concern persons of less *stature* than Lear; otherwise it will compete with the Lear line. But these conditions already point in the direction of a tale not too unlike Lear's, a tale of good son and bad son, a king-father deceived into fostering the bad and persecuting the good, until robbed of his kingdom by his illegitimate and evil son, even blinded by him, he learns at last the virtue of his good and legitimate son. It is the tale of the blind Paphlagonian king in Sidney's *Arcadia* (II, 10); and Shakespeare makes it into the story of Gloucester in *King Lear*.

We must note Shakespeare's very cunning strategy of representation in King Lear. Shakespeare is a great master of psychology; I don't mean this merely in its usual sense of his skillfully depicting his characters, but in the additional sense of his being very adroit in the manipulating of his audience. He knows that when people are extremely intent on something, a sudden interruption will be very startling; which is one reason why the knocking on the gate in Macbeth has such terrible force, for the audience is absorbed in the whispering murderers. He knows that a dreadful thing being done very quietly and slowly will seem all the more dreadful to an audience; which is one reason why Othello's coming to murder Desdemona is so powerful.

In King Lear he wants to arouse our sympathies with Lear to the utmost, and he knows that if we form an unfavorable opinion of someone who falls into misfortune we are far less sympathetic than if we had formed a favorable opinion of him. If, therefore, he can cause us first to look on Lear with some disfavor, and subsequently cause us to revise our opinions radically, he can work up our sympathetic emotions to an enormous pitch.

Look at what he allows us to see of Lear, step by step, and you will see how his strategy works. We *must not know too much about* Lear; we must see his faults first, then his virtues; and we must see his worse faults first, and then the lesser, and then the least; similarly, we must see his virtues in ascending order. Or rather I should say, what we *take* to be his faults; for many of his early actions as we get to know more of Lear are not what we took them for at all. To achieve this slow revelation Shakespeare uses the device of *ambiguous action*—that is, he invents actions for Lear, in the early part of the play, which on first sight look quite different from what they really are: his demand that his daughters profess their love publicly is, as I have interpreted it to you, the supreme example. His banishment of Cordelia is in any case a dreadful thing, but it is not a vicious moral action; it is a piece of folly, excusable in view of his character and his career.

It looks like a cold-hearted action; it is nothing of the sort; the underlying cause is his deep affection for Cordelia; in his view she has publicly slighted him, and he feels the wound terribly because those we love have power to hurt us most. Critics, even eminent ones, have been somewhat insensitive on this point; they have taken Lear's early acts all at face value, and criticized Shakespeare for making him arrogant or irascible or what-not. They have even criticized the play as beginning too abruptly, by contrast to the long introductory sequences in *Macbeth* or *Hamlet* or especially *Othello,* where the whole first act is nothing but introduction. But the reason for the difference is clear; in the other plays we must understand a great deal before the action begins, if the plot is to have its full effect; in *Lear,* on the other hand, if the plot is to have its full effect we must not know too much.

Shakespeare is not content simply to unfold gradually the character of Lear through his own actions; since so much of his behavior has to do with his interpretation of the characters of Goneril and Regan, they are gradually revealed to us as well. At first Lear seems to have but little ground for his resentment and anger, but as we know the sisters better we move into full accord with him. Why must Gloucester's eyes be put out on stage? It is a very horrible thing; but this is what Regan is capable of, and we must see it, not be told it, see with our own eyes exactly how it is done, to realize the full evil of her character. Why do she and her husband do it? Because Gloucester had a letter in his possession from Cordelia, whose forces had landed at Dover, and because Gloucester had helped the escape of Lear to Dover. If there was to be war the king had to be killed at once; Cornwall and Regan had already plotted his death; Gloucester had over-heard and frustrated it. It would have been no easy death; we can gather that from her tearing out parts of Gloucester's beard, her fierce questioning of him, her insistence that his other eye be gouged out; indeed, before he loses his own eyes, Gloucester says "I would not see thy cruel nails/ Pluck out his poor old eyes," and he is referring to Lear.

The character of Albany has never been much dis-cussed. Let me say one word about him. He has power to stop everything whenever he wishes; and we see him, in Act V, as the final agent of justice. Why does he not stop villainy and restore justice? Because, like the audience, he does not fully know; like the audi-ence, he regards Lear somewhat unfavorably at first, and gradually learns the truth. In other words, he is part of Shakespeare's general strategy of representa-tion; for the audience is moved also by the change in him.

IX
Phèdre

A GREAT GULF has existed, from the beginning, between
the French classical drama and the English-speaking
audience. John Dryden's *Essay of Dramatic Poesy,*
written in Racine's lifetime, makes it abundantly clear
that the gulf existed then and was wide; and in the
preface of the most recent translation of Racine—one
so new that it is still in process of being readied for
the press—the translator remarks sadly that devout
Anglo-Saxon Racinians have always been few and far
between, that outside that circle, a few have mere intellectual comprehension, and a great many *feel indifference or even hostility.* I am afraid he is right:
it seems to me that the gulf between us and Racine
is even greater than that between the French and
Shakespeare, and certainly greater than that between
us and the dramatists of antiquity whom the French
classicists took as their models. The standards of dramatic excellence and beauty differ for us and the
French; and the problem is that Racine must, it would
appear, be praised for qualities that we do not particularly esteem, while he is deficient in the qualities
that we hold highest.

217

We are apt to look a little coldly, for example, on the French dramatists' keeping of the unities of time, place, and action, especially when we find that they did not always do so, or that, in order to do it, like Corneille in *The Cid*, they had to crowd events quite implausibly into a single day. We find the plot slight and slow, the characterization thin, the speeches interminable, the diction flat; and we are not much cheered by being told that all this is because the French dramatists had certain conventions. It is somewhat like paying good money to see an acrobatic exhibition and finding only a man wriggling in a strait jacket. On complaining, we are told that, for a man in a strait jacket, he is a very fine acrobat, indeed.

Now, this attitude of ours will bear a little examination. In the first place, when it is not a mere mistaking of habit for preference—for many people suppose that they prefer something when they merely mean they are habituated to it—it is usually a mistaking of *quality* for *form*, or of *convention* for *form*. Our criticism of literature, and our casual talk about it as well, has for a very long time been *qualitative* rather than *formal*. That is, we have talked and do talk, about the qualities we want in poetry generally, or drama, generally, literature generally, even art generally; we want "high seriousness" or "wit" or originality or distinctiveness or some other *general* quality to be found in all works, regardless of their kind. We do not take into sufficient consideration the fact that the arts, while they have certain general principles in common, and even bear remarkable analogies to each other, chiefly depend upon principles peculiar to each art; that similarly, the so-called *literary* arts, while *they* have certain principles in common, *chiefly* depend upon principles peculiar to themselves. To say this another way: drama and lyric poetry may show certain analogies, but they are not one art; your great lyric poet—Keats, Shelley, Byron, Arnold, Tennyson, Swinburne—even when he has so pronounced a *dramatic* gift as Browning—is not necessarily a great, even a good dramatist. The reason for this is that quite different arts are involved—arts so different, in fact, that a great lyric poet is likely to fail in drama precisely through those qualities which make him great as a lyric poet. The point of this is simple: we ought not to demand of a given *kind* of work qualities which it is not the primary business of that kind of offer. Some people want "richness of diction" or "precision of imagery" or "complexity of texture"—for instance—in all works; but nothing is more obvious than that kinds of works exist —extremely valuable kinds—which would be ruined by the possession of these qualities. Do not misunderstand me; I am not saying there is anything wrong with qualitative criticism; Longinus, for example, is a qualitative critic, and a great one. But Longinus does not confuse quality with kind; it is that confusion which is wrong.

I have remarked that we also confuse convention with form, or—what amounts to the same thing— form with genre; for I define genre as form determined by conventional specification. This confusion is so habitual to us that it is very difficult to distinguish the things confused. Let me put it this way: conventions are kinds of *habits* of construction which have become associated with a given art; sooner or later they are usually elevated into *rules*. They are always supposed, in that case, to be part of the essence of the art, so that nothing beautiful or effective can be made in that art, supposedly, unless it is made in accordance with them; until some artist comes along and upsets the whole apple cart by making something obviously very beautiful which is also obviously not made in accordance with them. How often histories of music, for instance, tell us that Beethoven and Chopin smashed the forms and principles of music to give us a new music. Beethoven and Chopin did nothing of the sort; if they had "smashed the principles and forms" of music, they would have produced no music whatsoever. What they did was to break rules and conventions, and so escape from the genres which had been founded on these. For art does not depend on rule; there are no rules of art, unless you want to produce a work exactly like some previous work; art depends upon *principles*.

If these were simply theoretical considerations, I should not mention them here; but they have very important practical consequences, particularly for our attitude toward art. One who has been habituated to certain conventions often finds himself unable to comprehend a work which does not follow those conventions. In fact, while the work may be excellent, he may even be upset by it, if it departs radically from the conventions to which he is accustomed. The late Lord Dunsany, for instance—himself a talented writer and a man of conspicuously good taste—remained perplexed and irritated to the day of his death by the finest poems of the twentieth century. Be sure of one thing: unless you can see beyond conventions to the form itself, you will never come to a full comprehension or a proper appreciation of the work.

I suppose you have realized that all this is a prolog to a statement that we are a little cool to Racine because we are prevented from appreciation by the difference of conventions involved. Well, I shall now make that statement; but at the same time let me say that it doesn't help very much. The fact that something is different from what we think good does not prove that it is good—indeed, often enough, quite the contrary. There is little point, too, in admiring, as some critics have, the ease with which Racine handles the more rigid conventions; that is only our acrobat in the strait jacket. There is even less point, I think, in the tendency which T. S. Eliot seems to be following lately; if I follow him correctly, he is suggesting that the doctrine of the three unities is right and that we are wrong for not following it. I see only one way out of this. In all the arts our taste is absolutely prior; but when we suspect our taste in a given instance, or wish to confirm it, we must have recourse to principles. That is a noble passage in Sir Joshua Reynolds' *Discourses* in which he shows that conventions which are mutually repugnant, perhaps even contrary, can be understood and reconciled by reduction to their principle. His illustration, as I remember it, runs something like this: people of this nation doff their hats to show reverence; people of another, bow; still others genuflect; still others kneel; still others prostrate themselves. These customs seem incompatible with each other, until we realize that they all reduce to the same principle: that of indicating one's inferiority to the object of reverence by reducing, in token of it, one's bodily stature.

Let us, with Sir Joshua's procedure in mind, have a brief look at the chief differences between, say, the dramaturgy of Shakespeare and that of Racine.

Compare merely the *main* plot of any of Shakespeare's tragedies with the *plot* of any tragedy of Racine's, and you are struck with one thing immediately. The Shakespearian plot is far more *extensive* than the Racinian. I do not mean that it is more extensive in time, is likely to range over days, weeks, months even, whereas Racine's plots hold to a single day, though that is certainly true; I mean that it includes far more *incidents.* You can summarize the whole plot of a Racinian tragedy in a short paragraph; a summary of the main plot alone in a Shakespearian one will run into pages and still not be adequate. Indeed, some of Shakespeare's sub-plots, even, are in this sense more extensive than Racine's plots; the Gloucester *sub-plot* in *Lear,* for instance, contains more incidents than the *plot* of *Phèdre.*

There is another thing, however, which is not quite so obvious. Take any important scene in Shakespeare, look at it closely, and you will see that is is *compounded* of many *minor incidents.* To take a random example: the scene in which Gloucester is blinded. What happens in it? Cornwall, to whom Edmund has betrayed his father, asks Goneril to hasten to tell Albany that the French army has landed, and orders Gloucester apprehended. Regan wants to hang him at once. Goneril suggests the plucking out of his eyes.

Cornwall silences both and sends Edmund along with Goneril. Oswald comes to tell of Lear's escape to Dover. Cornwall decides the fate of Gloucester, implying that he will not be killed. Gloucester is brought in. He pleads, but is bound. Accused of treason, he denies it; Regan tears hairs from his beard; he rebukes her. Now he is interrogated. His answers enrage Cornwall and Regan; Cornwall puts out one eye. An old servant of Cornwall's rebels as Cornwall is about to put out the other. They fight, Cornwall is wounded; Regan stabs the servant from behind, killing him. The other eye is out. Gloucester in agony calls his son Edmund; Regan brutally discloses that it was Edmund who betrayed him. Gloucester realizes that he has unjustly suspected Edgar. Gloucester is thrust out of doors to wander blind. Cornwall announces his wound, withdraws to die. The servants discuss the atrocity they have witnessed; they decide to provide medicaments for him and to get Edgar, whom they know as Poor Tom, to guide him.

Compare this with a long scene in *Phèdre*. Phèdre comes in, very weak; she complains of the oppressiveness of her hair and clothing; her nurse rebukes her for captiousness; Phèdre speaks of her possible death, intimates that she has a wish for forests and chariots (a veiled reference to her love for Hippolyte); her cryptic discourse makes the nurse Oenone plead with her to disclose her secret; Oenone's accidental reference to Hippolyte makes Phèdre cry out. The nurse questions; Phèdre at last discloses that she loves Hippolyte, and tells the history of her love. I have stated this as fully as possible; even so, that statement betrays the simplicity of this scene. One event, really: Phèdre reveals the cause of her anguish as love for her stepson. Oenone questions, Phèdre answers; only the process on both sides is long drawn out.

But the number of incidents contained in the scene is not the only respect in which the Shakespearian scene is more complex. Shakespearian scenes are quite commonly crowded *with many characters,* whereas Racine's are not; and Shakespeare generally sets before us the *separate processes through which these many characters go* in the course of the scene. Our attention may not be upon them, but they are still alive and there, and responding in their own ways to whatever is happening. Let us look at the Gloucester scene again. We know the process of reaction of everyone in the scene, so long as he remains on stage; sometimes even beyond. When Gloucester is ordered to be brought, everyone is thinking of what may ensue. The brutal Regan, less cunning than her sister, is direct and thorough in her methods; she wants Gloucester hanged; Goneril, more insidious, wants his eyes plucked out; the cold Cornwall will consider. Edmund is silent. A significant silence; we know what it means; he has brought this about; he has what he wants. The servant who is to rebel does not speak as yet; a different silence. Follow the scene through; you will see that Shakespeare has had in mind each character's distinctive response to the event. Compare this with Act II, Scenes ii and iii of *Phèdre.* Scene ii: Aricie and Ismène are on stage; Hippolyte comes and reveals his love to Aricie. How does Ismène react to this? We do not know. How does Aricie react? Two words: *Quoi, seigneur!* What! my lord. Surprise. Scene iii: Théramène comes in and tells Hippolyte that Phèdre wishes to speak with him. Hippolyte asks Aricie whether he has declared his love in vain. She hints that he has not. This in the presence of Théramène and Ismène. How do these two react? Heaven knows. Put it this way: the French playwright's scenes are duets *alternando*; one character speaks, the other responds. Others are mute. Shakespeare's scenes are duets and trios and quartets and quintets, whole symphonies even.

The Shakespearian scene is more complex in yet another way. It is usually *highly circumstantial.* It usually occurs in a very definite place, of a highly distinctive character (read through Macbeth again and ask yourself how much you know about Macbeth's castle —you will surprise yourself); it occurs at a fairly precise time (go through Othello and notice how the hours of the day are distinguished). Ask yourself how the characters are dressed, what objects are about them, how they react to these circumstances; you will be amazed; and you will notice that the circumstances are always carefully chosen to enhance the special emotional effect of each scene.

Now look at Racine. Under the cast of characters of *Phèdre* you will find: "The scene is Troezen, a city in the Peloponnese." That is the place, and that is all. What time is it? Well, in Act I, Scene iii Phèdre addresses the sun; so it is day. And that is about all. Shakespeare's world is definite and clear, we see the interactions between nature and the works of man, we see how different men respond to the different surroundings (think of Duncan and Banquo coming to

Macbeth's castle, Act I, Scene vi). Racine's action takes place in a blank of space, a blank of time. One thinks of some cold abstract pavilion in eternity; or rather, one does not really think of it at all.

Notice, too, the extreme *particularization,* I should say almost individualization of Shakespeare's characters—their temperaments, their moral principles, their passions, their thoughts. They have definite habits, quirks, predilections. We know a good deal of what they are, and we know their earlier history. Look at Hamlet: he is not merely a scholar in the abstract; he constantly sees life as a scholar would see it. At a moment of supreme anguish and distraction he talks in terms of books, because thoughts about books, tablets, writing and erasing, notes and commentaries have become habitual to him:

> Remember thee!
> Yea, from the table of my memory
> I'll wipe away all trivial fond records,
> All saws of books, all forms, all pressures past
> That youth and observation copied there
> And thy commandment all alone shall live
> Within the book and volume of my brain
>
> .   .   .   .
>
> My tables—meet it is I set it down
> That one may smile and smile and be a villain.
> .   .   .   .

What else do we know about him? A thousand things, from his love of plays and players to his interests in music and poetry and his skill in fencing; he thinks in terms of these, and acts in terms of these.

What do we know of Phèdre in Racine? In a very

general way, her character, her situation, her feelings.

Now consider that at important moments in Shake-spearian tragedy we are shown the major characters, at least, in a *highly complex way*. All their faculties are energized and in constant interplay, even in conflict, so that one dominates now, the other presently; sensation affects memory, memory imagination, imagination passion, passion thought. Look at the great soliloquy of *Hamlet*, Act II, Scene ii, which is only less famous than the "To be or not to be" speech, and ask yourself what is going on in Hamlet's mind, and of how much of it he is aware, and of how much he is unaware; and this will be perfectly clear to you. Compare it with Phèdre's soliloquy, Act IV, Scene v; in it we see only the movement of her thought, and her consequent feelings, and all this very generally. She does not, like Hamlet, become so choked with passion that she cannot speak or think; her imagination does not run away with her reason; she does not indicate her private detestations which have nothing to do with the situation in hand; she does not draw upon her reading, or for that matter, her past history. Her speech is an eloquent and moving one; she herself is deeply moved; but it is poles apart from that equally moving and eloquent soliloquy of Hamlet's.

Let me very briefly list a few more striking differences. Shakespeare mixes comic scenes and characters with his most serious actions; Racine does not. Shakespeare builds elaborate sub-plots and by-plots, and uses them very variously: to achieve suspense or the unexpected, to contrast his main character and his actions with courses of action open to other characters (compare Hamlet with Fortinbras and Laertes, compare Lear with Gloucester), and for many other purposes. Racine does not use sub-plots at all. Shakespeare, if he has to effect dramatic exposition of any length, will always cast it into a kind of story interesting in itself, with characters sometimes especially constructed to carry on that story; look at the ghost story we are given in *Hamlet,* long before the action proper begins; the witch tale we are given long before Duncan is murdered; to say nothing of the story in the whole first act of *Othello*. Racine will do nothing of the sort. He wants his exposition over in a hurry; he reduces the characters who have to do it to mere stock functionaries, such as confidants and messengers and such; they tell or are told what is necessary, and get out of the way. Emphasis is on the principal characters only.

Enough of these differences, now; there are many more; but what we have must suffice. Why do we have these differences?

Well, we can give a good number of historical reasons. The English theatre was popular, the French aristocratic; the one had to please all strata of society, the other only one. The English consequently mingled comic structures and devices with tragic, comic matter with serious; the French kept them separate. The French tended to model closely upon the works of antiquity; the English did not. The French also took subjects, therefore, which might be worked into such forms; the English took their subjects anywhere and everywhere. And so on. We can perhaps explain the differences of artistic practice in this way, but if we are to see the practices as genuinely *artistic* practices

228

we must find *artistic* reasons for them. These are the primary reasons, anyway, why the artist as *artist* engages in them.

It should be clear from this comparison that Shakespeare is concerned with long successions of events, Racine with briefer ones; that is, that Shakespeare is concerned with processes, Racine with situations. Shakespeare individualizes, particularizes, circumstantializes; Racine generalizes. Shakespeare correlates action with action, character with character; Racine selects. Shakespeare examines a highly individual action in a universal context of its correlatives; Racine is concerned with the universalized act in itself. The technique of Shakespeare is that of aggregation; the technique of Racine, like that of the ancients on whom he modelled, is that of isolation. Only with this difference: the ancients had the technique of isolation forced upon them by the meager dramatic means at hand; Racine adopts it as a deliberate device, for the sake of the values it has.

Shakespeare studies the whole complex of issues about a given issue, and that issue is given meaning by its complex relations. Take *King Lear*; it turns on the major issue of self-love versus love for others. Shakespeare explores *all* familial relations (father-daughter, daughter-father, father-son, son-father, husband-wife, wife-husband, etc.) *all* social relations (friend-friend, equal-equal, inferior-superior, etc.) *all* economic relations (master-servant, servant-master) and all political relations (king-subject, lord-vassal, etc.). Racine studies the major issue in itself; refined to its essence, made as universal as possible, separate from any qualification of circumstance, apart from its cor-relatives. And of course this difference affects the very devices these poets must use. Let me take only one example, because otherwise that would be a very long story. Shakespeare can mingle comedy with tragedy (I am using the vulgar phrase here, which is inaccurate) whereas Racine cannot. Why? Because if a given par-ticular incident, in itself, is both tragic and comic, the comedy weakens the tragic effect; Racine, who focusses on the single action or situation, consequently cannot employ comic elements. If, however, emphasis is on the succession of events, rather than the single event, even the ridiculous may pave the way to greater terror. Look at the so-called comic relief scenes in Shake-speare; they may be comic in abstraction from the play; they are not in context; who ever laughed during the porter scene in *Macbeth,* or the gravedigger scene in *Hamlet?* Incidentally, if a dramatist is going to focus on a single event, or at any rate an extremely short sequence, he is likely to find the three unities of ac-tion, place, and time indispensable; if not, he will find them a hindrance; and perhaps *that* explains *that.*

We see then two opposite methods: the Shakespear-ian method of enriching, the Racinian of refining. We are well aware of the value of the first; what about that of the second?

The real difference between these two contrasting methods lies in the way in which each engages the minds of the spectators; that is, which of the mental faculties each engages first, what others it involves, and what the ultimate engagement is. To reduce this to the simplest possible illustration: everyone has at some time recounted his own experiences to others, and has at one time or another used each of these methods. Think back to what you were trying to do in your narrative, and you will see that, perhaps unconsciously, you used the method best fitted to achieve your end. If you were trying to make the story as credible as possible, and as emotionally moving as possible, you had to address yourself to the *imagination* of your listener; for whatever is very vividly imagined is likely to pass unquestioned, and also, it is likely to arouse one's emotions strongly; indeed, it is a kind of general law in human nature that we are moved emotionally most strongly by our sensations (what we see, hear, etc.); a little less, by our imaginations; hardly at all, by our abstract intellectual conceptions. Take an airplane accident, for instance; you are most strongly moved if you witness it; next, if you imagine it (and here everything depends on how vividly you imagine it—if you imagine it with a vividness approaching that of actual sensation, you will be greatly moved, while if you imagine it very faintly, you will be moved only slightly); finally, the mere abstract notion of such an accident, totally apart from questions of the possibility of its happening, of whom it is happening to, and from all circumstance, is as little moving as possible. But notice something: the utmost possible vividness of imagination approaches the clarity of sensation; at this time, however, the idea is as obscure as possible, for sensation is at the farthest possible remove from the intellect and its ideas; whereas, the farther we move away from sensation and vivid imagination, the clearer grow our ideas. So that, if you tell an experience of

yours with the wish to make your listener realize as
clearly as possible, not the circumstances, but the principles or issues involved in it, you will leave out all
circumstance, you will make the experience almost a
transparency through which those principles or issues
can be seen. Shakespeare's methods stimulate emotion
and imagination to the utmost; but they do not make
the central issues as clear as possible; witness the many
dissonant interpretations critics have given us of *Hamlet* or *King Lear*. The methods of Racine, on the other
hand, set these principles and issues almost nakedly
before us. The universal is of course always in Shakespeare, but we have to win our way toward it through
circumstance and accident, just as we win our way
toward experience and wisdom and science in life;
Racine proposes the universal to us directly.

Let us look at his dramatic method in *Phèdre* a little
more closely. As you doubtless know, this play is
founded upon the *Hippolytus* of Euripides and the
Hippolytus of Seneca; and to a degree Racine also
models upon Euripides and Seneca. I say *to a degree*
because we can make far too much of that. In the first
place, Racine, like other French classic dramatists,
feels quite free to drop any elements of ancient drama
which seem ineffective to him. Like others, he realizes
that the Chorus, though imposed on Greek tragedy by
its origin in choric forms, is no essential part of tragedy; in fact, it is likely to be embarrassing dramatically; not only does it from time to time hold up the
action for the sake of a lyric interlude; but, more important, even if it is used dramatically and as a real
character in the play it presents the dramatist with

the irritating problem of a character who must remain on stage continuously and for the greater part of the action. Consequently, Racine uses the Chorus only in his two Biblical plays, *Esther* and *Athalie;* even there, he gives it quite different employment. As with the Chorus, so with other dramatic devices and conventions of antiquity; he uses them only when they are effective for his purposes, and insofar as they are useful.

What is more important still, while he will keep as closely as he may to the subject matter of his models, or to ancient traditions surrounding these, he feels perfectly free to reconceive that subject matter, to omit, alter, or add in any way that may bring him closer to the universal, the essential action. Compare him with Euripides and Seneca, and you see this at once. In Euripides, the action of the *Hippolytus* is as follows: Aphrodite, insulted because Hippolytus prefers to worship Artemis and will not worship her, plans her revenge: Phaedra is to love her stepson Hippolytus, her husband Theseus is to learn of this, and in rage to destroy his son. This happens as follows: Phaedra, pressed by her nurse, reveals to her that she is tormented by love for her stepson, and that she has determined to die for the sake of her honor. The nurse reveals the secret to Hippolytus, who is horrified. Phaedra learns of that revelation and hangs herself. At this point Theseus returns from his travels, hears of Phaedra's suicide; on investigating he finds tied to her wrist a letter she has written, accusing Hippolytus of violating her. Enraged, and unconvinced by the innocent Hippolytus' protests, he calls down the wrath of Poseidon the sea-god upon his son. The boy, bound by oath not to reveal the truth, goes into exile. Shortly afterward, a messenger comes with the announcement that Hippolytus is dying; the sea-god had sent up a monstrous bull from the sea, which terrified the horses pulling the boy's chariot; the chariot was broken, the boy was dragged. Theseus rejoices, and desires to see his son's sufferings; but the goddess Artemis appears and reveals the boy's innocence and Phaedra's guilt. Theseus watches in grief as his son dies.

In Seneca the story is a little different. Phaedra, at first about to yield to her unlawful love, is dissuaded by her nurse; she resolves on death instead. On meeting Hippolytus she faints, and he catches her; in his arms she reveals her love. He is about to kill her, but throws away his sword and goes away. The nurse, to save her mistress' honor, gives out that Hippolytus has violated Phaedra. Theseus returns and inquires, and Phaedra also accuses Hippolytus by implication. Theseus, enraged, invokes the wrath of the sea-god upon his son; the boy is dragged by his horse, much as before, and killed. Phaedra then reveals the truth to Theseus and kills herself.

Racine makes numerous changes. Hippolyte is in love with Aricie, last survivor of a family hateful to Thésée, who has bidden her live without marriage, so that the family will die with her. Thésée is away, his whereabouts unknown. Phèdre near dying reveals her love to the nurse. A waiting woman brings the news that Thésée is dead. The nurse, at first horrified by Phèdre's passion, now regards it as blameless, and persuades her to live. Phèdre now reveals her love to Hippolyte, who recoils in horror; she asks the nurse to act as intercessor between them. The nurse presently brings the news that Thésée is still alive and will shortly appear; she urges Phèdre to accuse Hippolyte to preserve her own honor. Phèdre, distracted, yields. When Thésée arrives, Phèdre refuses to embrace him and speaks of her shame. The nurse calumniates the son to his father; Thésée invokes the sea-god's wrath upon Hippolyte. When Phèdre is about to intercede, she is stunned by the news that Hippolyte loves Aricie. On speaking with the nurse she realizes the full horror of her action. Thésée is beginning to regret his curse upon his son, to suspect that it was not wholly just, when news is brought him of Hippolyte's death. He announces it to Phèdre. She has poisoned herself; she clears Hippolyte with her dying words.

Notice the effect of these changes. Phaedra is made the full center of the play; she, not Theseus, is the real agent of the tragic deed; at the same time, the actual calumniation is shifted from her to the nurse, too base an act for her own character. Hippolytus, too perfect for tragic purposes, is given the slight fault of loving his father's enemy, Aricia. Theseus is reported dead, to permit Phaedra a disclosure to Hippolytus which she would not otherwise have made. In short, Racine has removed whatever was odious, out of character, or improbable in Euripides and Seneca, and refined and distilled until he has the perfect tragic essence of the subject.

Why then, you may ask, does he follow the tragic myth at all, as in the case of the sea-monster and one or two other matters? Why does he keep the ancient names? In order to make the action remote in time, to take from it all immediacy; as in *Bajazet* he uses contemporary events remote in space; both for the same reason, to universalize the story. Shakespeare makes his actions and character immediate, by circumstance; Racine makes them remote.

It is not that he denies all emotion to his drama. Indeed, they are powerful dramas emotionally. But he will not permit emotion to be excited at the expense of a *clear moral judgment* of the characters and their actions. In precisely the same fashion, he breaks with Rotrou and Corneille and his other precursors by taking the emphasis from *action as action* and placing it upon action as the consequence of thought. The dianoetic tragedy, the tragedy of thinking and reasoning, is his great innovation in French classical drama; the tragic figures bring their misfortunes upon themselves through the principles they hold and the consequences which they draw from them. Since that reasoning must at all times be rendered as clear as possible to the audience, Racine must generally forego image, metaphor, and most of the devices which we so strongly associate with poetry; for these stimulate our imagination but distract us from the thought itself, or as in the case of metaphor, are ambiguous and do not set the thought clearly before us.

X
Modern Drama and Tragedy

DO WE HAVE TRAGEDY in modern times? If so, of what sort is it? If not, why not? And what difference does it make?

The best way to answer these questions is consider some specimens. *Mourning Becomes Electra* strikes me as excellent for our purposes, for a number of reasons. It is often called O'Neill's supreme achievement; O'Neill himself has the reputation of being among the most serious of modern dramatists—indeed, he is often spoken of as America's first real tragic dramatist; and he founded his trilogy upon the legends which underlie the *Oresteia*.

I suppose that nobody of any sense goes around with complete summaries of plots in his head; so it will be well to recall what happens in *Mourning Becomes Electra*. We had better recall O'Neill's purpose first: he was trying to write a modern psychological drama, with some approximation to the Greek sense of fate, so that an audience which no longer believed in gods or supernatural retribution might still have something like that sense, and be moved accordingly. For a number of very good reasons which we need not go into, he set his trilogy in New England. The Trojan War became the Civil War. He gave his characters names somewhat resembling those of their Greek prototypes: Agamemnon became Asa Mannon, ultimately Ezra Mannon; Clytemnestra became Christine; Electra became Eleanor, Ellen, Elsa, Laodicea, and finally Lavinia; Orestes became Orin, and Aegisthus became Adam.

O'Neill had more in mind than a modernization of the Greeks; he was also trying to remedy what he took to be a deficiency in Greek drama. Electra, he felt, had been allowed to "peter out . . . into married life," as he puts it. Why was there no Greek play about her after the death of Clytemnestra? Why should she be exempt from retribution? Pursuit of these questions led him to make her the central figure of his drama, and the emphasis is reflected in the title.

Homecoming, The Hunted, and *The Haunted* make up the three plays of *Mourning Becomes Electra*. In *Homecoming,* Christine, who has been having a liaison with Adam Brant, awaits the return of her husband from the war. Lavinia, herself secretly in love with Adam, has discovered the liaison and tells her mother that it must be broken off. Christine plots with Adam to poison Ezra. On the morning after his homecoming Ezra and Christine quarrel, Ezra has a heart attack, and Christine gives him poison instead of his heart medicine. Lavinia discovers the poison bottle, surmises what has happened, and determines on revenge.

In *The Hunted* Orin returns. Always greatly attached to his mother, he grows jealous of Adam. Under

Lavinia's urgings his feelings grow more violent; ultimately, having tracked Christine to Adam's ship and discovered their rendezvous, he shoots Adam after his mother has departed. The murder is taken to be the deed of ship-robbers; but Lavinia and Orin disclose the truth to Christine, as well as their knowledge of her guilt. Christine commits suicide.

In *The Haunted* Lavinia, who has come to resemble her mother more and more, becomes the object of Orin's strange affection. Orin ultimately recognizes this as incestuous desire for both her and his mother. He proposes incestuous relations to Lavinia. When she rejects him in horror, he kills himself. Lavinia herself at last realizes that her attachment to her fiancé is nothing but her desire for the dead Adam; she frightens off her lover and gives herself over to a life as a recluse, to suffer the tortures of remorse until her death.

This brief summary does more than the usual injustice done by such things, but perhaps it will serve our purposes. O'Neill has the Greeks in mind, is even vying with them, and invites comparison with them. Well, then: how does *Mourning Becomes Electra* compare with the *Oresteia?*

Atreus and Thyestes are here represented by two persons outside the play, Grandfather Abe Mannon and his brother David. There is no banquet; simply, both brothers are in love with the same woman, Marie Brantôme (Acrope as a Canuck nurse-girl); and when David wins her, Abe in revenge cheats David out of his share of the estate, and the lovers, along with their son Adam, suffer extreme poverty. David is a drunkard and weakling; when Adam grows up, he comes to detest the very name of Mannon and adopts his mother's name in the shortened version of Brant. He enters into the play, thus, quasi-incognito. He seduces Christine in vengeance against the Mannons but falls in love with her. He agrees to help in the murder of Ezra—his help consists in procuring the poison—partly because he wants Christine, partly because he wants revenge against Ezra, partly because he wants a ship.

Even this much suggests a general debasement of character, motive, and action; and further examination establishes it beyond doubt. What is the difference between Clytemnestra and Christine, Agamemnon and Ezra Mannon, Electra and Lavinia, Orestes and Orin? The Aeschylean figures are all of an imposing stature; O'Neill's are not. As against the superb and "manly-minded" Clytemnestra, Christine is weak, cowardly, irresolute, spiteful, and wholly the puppet of her emotions and desires. Clytemnestra kills out of a whole complex of powerful motives, as we know; Christine kills because Ezra disgusts her and Adam attracts her. Clytemnestra *must* kill; I have never been convinced that Christine has sufficient reason to. Clytemnestra commits a violent and daring murder, and makes a bold and triumphant avowal of it. Christine treacherously poisons a sick man, already helpless in a paroxysm, and seeks to conceal her crime. We do not approve of Clytemnestra's crime, but we are compelled to respect her in the doing of it; we have the sense that horrible as her deed is, she thinks of it in some strange way as just and right. But it is impossible to have any respect whatsoever for Christine. In the whole history of literature we find no other woman

who can match—in her special way—the Clytemnestra
of Aeschylus; not even Lady Macbeth. But we have
met Christines in countless melodramas, and the police
courts find her a very familiar figure indeed.

Orin and Lavinia are similarly debasements of their
prototypes. Orestes commits actual matricide, in horror and revulsion, under divine direction; Orin is a
psychotic, moved by unconscious incestuous desires;
and his guilt in his mother's death is merely fancied.
Electra suffers dishonor, privation, and oppression,
sees her people laboring under tyranny, and her father's murderers flourishing unpunished; she acts to
restore justice. Lavinia is a girl cheated of her love by
her mother. True, O'Neill penetrates the moral pre-
texts of his characters, to reveal them as merely animal drives; but that penetration is itself a debasement. One cannot dignify human beings by regarding
them as animals.

Suppose, then, that there are these debasements.
What does it matter?

It matters a very great deal, so far as the seriousness
of the action is concerned. O'Neill supposed that the
seriousness of Greek tragedy depended upon belief in
the gods, in divine intervention and retribution. He
was completely mistaken. We regard as serious whatever can importantly affect our happiness or misery;
whatever can give great pleasure or pain, mental or
physical; whatever similarly affects the happiness or
pleasure of those for whom we have some concern,
or of a good number of people, or of people whom we
take to be of considerable worth; or whatever involves
a principle upon which all such things depend; or

anything that bears a sufficient resemblance to these, or a sufficient relation. In our discussion of the *Agamemnon* we saw that every one of these elements of seriousness was involved in the action and that the poet used every device to give us the *sense* of their importance. It is that sense of tremendous importance which is effective, not the theology; and the proof of this is that "an intelligent audience of today, possessed of no belief in gods or supernatural retribution"—I am quoting O'Neill's description of the audience he thought he was addressing—is still profoundly moved by the Aeschylean drama.

And consequently the substitution of believed Freudian doctrines for unbelieved theology will not work. Such beliefs can have no great emotive force in themselves. They can affect us only as they relate to things which do have such force, to things which already embody the values of which I have been speaking. An animal drive or impulse, no matter how firmly we are convinced of its existence, can only affect us through our reflection on its capacity to produce goods and evils of a certain nature, magnitude, and duration.

O'Neill's trilogy, thus, can have only limited seriousness. The misfortunes are confined to a single family, affecting the fate of no one outside it. They are not conceived as involving any principle upon which the happiness of all of us or most of us must depend. They do not even *resemble* anything likely to happen to any great number of us. And they do not happen to persons whom we value highly. They can only affect us as they play upon our philanthropic feelings; and O'Neill, in so limited a dramatic conception, can only move us by insisting upon the intensity of the suffering of his characters. I am not at all sure that he himself knows *what* they feel; certainly we do not; perhaps all that anyone knows is that the Mannons are having a rather bad time.

I must conclude, therefore, that if tragedy displays an action of the utmost seriousness and significance, *Mourning Becomes Electra* is not a tragedy. I am not saying that it should have been tragedy or even that I am sorry it is not tragedy. I am simply saying that it is not. Yet, as I said earlier, a work seems always to make a proposal. I cannot avoid the feeling here that O'Neill somehow proposed something of tragic quality and that he failed because he failed to comprehend what was supremely serious and significant.

It is impossible to look at modern drama—by which I mean drama from Ibsen's day to the present—without being struck by its richness and variety. There have been other periods of expansion in the history of drama, but I do not think it can be claimed that the Age of Elizabeth or the *Siglo de Oro,* for instance, produced plays of such diversity as the modern period. In the latter we find an immense and rapid proliferation of forms, coupled with the discovery and successful employment of new devices and techniques. There is a swift and steady expansion of the subject matter of drama; new materials are introduced, a fresh significance is found in old ones, and both are handled to produce the most subtle differentiations of effect. There are many evidences, along with all this, of basic reconceptions of the drama—of what the "dramatic" consists in, of the ends and effects of drama, even of the very nature of the theatre itself.

The gains are obvious. Are there any losses? I think we must admit there have been. If modern drama exhibits a remarkable expansion, there has also been a certain contraction. Verse has practically disappeared from modern drama; despite certain notable exceptions, it is a prose drama. And the prose—again with certain exceptions—is no greatly varied prose. On the contrary, it has shown a tendency to become more and more like ordinary speech, or rather, more and more like the ordinary speech of the man who is a little less than the ordinary. The drama has increasingly sought to be articulate in the language of the inarticulate; and because it has done so, it has had to confine itself to such subject matter as its language might permit. The language of the inarticulate does not permit the expression of subtle or profound thought or emotion; consequently drama has had to forego the subtler and profounder thoughts and emotions. And since language and thought and emotion enter into the subtler expressions of character, drama has had to forego the latter as well.

You may test these statements very easily. Open an anthology of Elizabethan drama and leaf through. You will quickly see that there are great differences between the styles of Marlowe, Shakespeare, Webster, Tourneur, and Middleton. You will notice a very extensive vocabulary and greatly diversified grammatical constructions. Read almost any of the plays; you will find that the major characters, at least, have their distinctive manners of speaking and that different social classes speak differently. Read a speech of any length by a major character; you will usually find that you are told a great deal about what he is thinking and feeling, what sort of person he is, and sometimes even what is going on in the remoter corners of his mind. Now pick up an anthology of modern drama, and repeat the process. The case will now be abundantly clear to you. If not, push the experiment a step farther: try to identify dramatists, plays, and characters *simply by reference to the language.* I think you will succeed in this far better with the Elizabethans than with the moderns.

I do not want to insist on the *necessity* for drama of a great variety of styles, though that variety is obviously useful. The French Classical dramatists exhibit a far narrower range of styles than the Elizabethans, but they exhibit language of very great *flexibility.* And, if you are to have any really wide variation of fine drama, you must have stylistic variety or stylistic flexibility. You cannot play Beethoven's Opus 111 on a child's five-note piano; and you cannot display the full range of character, thought, and passion in a language founded upon what the ordinary man thinks, feels, and says in an ordinary situation. Humanity simply will not translate into such sub-Basic English. The problems of translating Aeschylus are nothing by comparison.

Modern drama has evolved, as I said, an immense variety of devices and techniques; but even here the critic who is willing to be sufficiently captious (as I, for one, happen to be) can protest that there is some restriction. Almost all of these devices have the same general tendency to decrease the distance between actors and audiences, to give a greater impression of immediacy or a greater continuity of the drama with life or—in a word—to commit the drama to greater and greater realism.

That realism, now that we have tracked it down, lies at the bottom of most dramatic construction. I am afraid that it is a very narrow realism. It takes as the model of reality the common probabilities of everyday life, as that life is lived by persons much like ourselves. It has developed, of course, out of the naturalism and realism of the nineteenth century, the "cup and saucer realism," "the slice of life." That naturalism grew out of a protest against certain artificialities in drama and fiction, and proclaimed itself, in contrast, an exponent of truth. From the very first, of course, it has had to depart from that "truth." No playgoer or novel-reader is so imbecile as to pay for the privilege of observing what he may witness at any time, free of charge, by sitting in a park, walking up a back stair, or poking his head out of a window. The unusual had to be introduced, for the plain reason that the usual is likely to be uninteresting. The characters had to be seen at a time of crisis, and the audience had to have a view of them which ordinary life does not usually afford at such a time—the view, as H. L. Mencken once put it, through "the terrifying key-hole." People like the Alvings and Gablers and Helmers do not often exhibit their anguish in public.

As a program for new art, realism was undoubtedly fruitful: it would take us a long time to read the roll-call of the great fiction and drama which came out of it. As a program for new art, moreover, it extended the arts of fiction and drama. But it was never intended as, and cannot possibly serve as, a program for all art. Nevertheless, that is the role it is gradually coming to fill—quietly, unofficially, as a matter of assumption and custom rather than of rational decision. In this role it may become quite as tyrannical for drama as the conventions it was devised to attack.

We can see something of its stringency in two ways: we can ask to what extent it is actually commensurate with life, and we can ask to what extent it is commensurate with art. I do not think it can be claimed that modern drama as a whole—I have in mind not merely American contemporary drama, but European as well, and that from Ibsen onward—has managed to catch anything like a total image of life. Wonderfully as it has caught particular aspects, aspects never caught and never seen so before, I find that it has not caught certain others of high importance. I shall leave that matter, however, to your decision. It involves the question of what life is, and there are so many different conceptions of that, no doubt, that the matter is hardly arguable. But the extent to which modern drama is commensurate with art is a simple matter; we have only to look at what has been done in the past that might still be valuable and ask ourselves whether we are doing it. Such a look will establish at once that we are not doing quite a lot of valuable things that have been done in the past. One that particularly interests me is this: we are not producing tragedy.

Tragedy involves characters who are, as Aristotle says, "better than we are"—better than the ordinary

247

man. He meant *morally—of greater worth;* but the notion of superiority naturally associated itself, in societies which drew sharp and extreme distinctions not merely between persons but between the kinds of lives they were permitted to lead, with the notion of superiority of rank; and this association was turned into rigid rule by theorists like Donatus, who laid down the pattern of the theory of tragedy which was to be transmitted through the Middle Ages to the Renaissance. Even in the Renaissance, however, there sprang up a species of domestic tragedy, a "tragedy of the ordinary man," the leading examples of which are *The Yorkshire Tragedy* and *Arden of Feversham.* This species came to particular prominence and popularity later in the plays of George Lillo and others, and our contemporary tragedies of the ordinary man are descendants of this line.

These domestic tragedies had, and continue to have, the very great value of exhibiting the seriousness even of humble life, and the far greater value of extending the range of our sympathy—that is, of engaging our sympathies for someone with whom we might not otherwise have sympathized. The older forms patterned themselves for the most part upon high tragedy, except that they dealt with persons of lower station, and had to make various adjustments accordingly. The plots are general analogs of those of high tragedy; but character, motive, and circumstance are altered. *The Fatal Curiosity,* for example, turns on one of the stock forms of tragic deed, the killing of a stranger who is subsequently discovered to be a relative; only here the father murders for money, under the extreme pressure of poverty. Later forms depend, for their effect, on other elements of the serious. A play like Arthur Miller's *Death of a Salesman* achieves its seriousness through the fact that Willy Loman's situation is representative of, or at any rate analogous to, the situation of so many people. Tennessee Williams' plays depend for their power upon extremity of suffering and the invention of characters particularly sensitive and vulnerable to a particular kind of torment. Yet others—like Miller's *The Crucible,* which I think is one of the closest modern approximations to tragedy —achieve their effect through the importance of the moral issues involved.

It seems, in a way, ridiculous to talk about the dangers of such forms. Any artistic endeavor must involve its dangers; tragedy can turn into bombastic fustian, comedy into inanity or vulgarity. The excellent artist will do excellent things, and the bad one will do bad things, in any case. On the other hand, modern serious drama seems, at times, almost innocent of the dangers to which it is particularly liable; and we may as well consider what they are. It is concerned with the ordinary man, and primarily with the suffering of the ordinary man; and in order to make that suffering important, it must intensify the anguish of its protagonist. In its endeavor to obtain sympathy it can readily fall into sentimentality or morbidity. There is no special merit in displaying or observing suffering. After the rebellion of Spartacus, six thousand persons, men, women, and children, were crucified along both sides of the Appian Way, extending far out into the suburbs of Rome; and the Romans took little sightseeing trips with their families, to watch anguish which must have been acute. I do not think there was anything very meritorious in this behavior of the Romans. And I do not think there would be anything very meritorious in our walking into a cancer ward or a lunatic asylum, where people are suffering the absolutes of physical or mental torture, simply so that we might observe their agony and sympathize with it. To return to drama: unless the dramatist can give us a significant perception—one that evokes in us a response of some merit—he had better not show us the suffering at all. It can only be painful to us, or, if not painful, pleasurable in a way that is worse for us than the pain would be.

Another danger is violence. Stringent realism of dialog—particularly when it is the language of the inarticulate—does not allow of the expression of intense or deep emotion, as I have said; consequently we must see dreadful things done physically to the characters, or emotion must exhibit itself in violent physical action. What can characters of this sort do to show their rage or their suffering, except to slam doors and smash crockery and beat their fists upon wall or table, what can they do except rant in the clichés of common speech?

Put it this way: by all means let us have the ordinary man. But let us by no means have an ordinary view of the ordinary man; and even then, let us not suppose that there can be nothing else. Much of it is fine drama, and it is serious.

But I do not think it is of the highest seriousness; I do not think it is tragedy.

At this point I can imagine an impatient reader who says, *All right, you want an action of the highest seriousness, and I suppose you want verse and fine diction. What about "Murder in the Cathedral"?*

Murder in the Cathedral is a very nice piece of work. It is what is called a period piece, and the costumes of the period are bound to be pleasing. Nearly everyone likes even ordinary medieval dress, to say nothing of Archbishop's robes and knightly armor and priestly vestments; and the costumes of the Four Tempters offer very pleasant opportunities for the costumier's fantasy. Its subject is an event that everyone would agree was serious and important. The poetry itself is quite beautiful, it helps rather than hinders the play, and gives at times a pleasant feeling that something profound is being said. It has the even greater merit of not being utterly ridiculous when spoken on the stage, which is a merit that many modern poetic dramatists have striven for in vain.

Having now been quite handsomely fair, I feel that I have built up a certain amount of what the hero of a recent novel calls *moral credit*. The hero in question builds up such credit so that he can draw upon it, to cover any subsequent sins; and like him, I now propose to draw on mine. Is *Murder in the Cathedral* a real *play*, or is it rather a *poem* of some kind which becomes more effective when recited, with suitable gestures, by actors in costume?

I have argued at considerable length that in a play the action or plot must be the main thing, and that it, and not some subsidiary part, should be primarily responsible for the effect upon us. Suppose we look at the action here. In the first place, what about this martyrdom? Is it a triumph? In what way? Why was it morally necessary for Becket—not the historical Becket but the Becket of the play? Was his situation such that his continuing to live really affected the fortunes of the Church? Why should he have made it so easy for the Knights to kill him? What is there in his actions to convince us that, whatever the purity of his motives, he is not following a wrong-headed course of action? Doubtless I am talking something like the Knights; I may well be; but let me say that, whatever the case may have been in the historical event, in the *play* the Knights have at least this much point, that the dramatist has failed to make Becket's act what it should be, a patently right course of action. It may be objected that the play assumes that we will stand on the side of Christianity and the Church; in which case I retort that it is none of the dramatist's business which side we are on. It is his business to make a play that will stand on its own legs. The cheap popular writer, for the sake of a quick and easy effect, may hook on to any belief or predisposition of his public, even very ephemeral ones, for these will not be so ephemeral as his work; but the serious artist must anchor his foundations in human nature itself; no work of art can survive the foundations on which it is built.

Second, is this all there is to martyrdom and sainthood? One quite calmly makes up one's mind to get killed, and gets killed? No anguish, no mortal terrors, no sweats? Even Christ went through his Gethsemane —but Becket does not. I do not know much about

sainthood, but I do know something of the trials and
tribulations of becoming a full professor; and I know
that Eliot makes sainthood far easier of achievement.
The murder of Becket is, in history, a tremendous
human drama, pregnant with grave issues, charged
with passion; it seems to me that Eliot has but a
shallow and tepid conception of it. I find no situation
realized here and no character realized. The characters
are different aspects of Eliot's mind; they are participants in a discourse within his mind, not distinct dramatic entities. The Knights themselves are only Eliot
stating his idea ironically.

If Eliot fails to make a true dramatic action charged
with its own proper power, he uses certain devices to
give the illusion that he has made such an action. The
most notable is the discussion of Becket with his
Tempters. I have just said that all of Eliot's characters
are only participants in a discourse within Eliot's
mind; the Four Tempters are precisely that, within
Becket's mind. They are no more real characters than,
let us say, Soul and Body in the various medieval de-
bates between soul and body; they are simply an internal conflict externalized in metaphor. Even in the
treatment of this segment—a rather considerable segment of the action—Eliot shows his characteristic dramatic weakness. The conflict is not much of a conflict,
the Tempters haven't a ghost of a chance, Becket wins
over them easily and without turning a hair. Truly
Eliot's saints show but a fugitive and cloistered virtue,
and they win their immortal garlands quite without
dust and heat. Here, let us notice, the Tempters are
simply four personifications of four courses of action

which lie open to Becket. Three of them he has already rejected; the fourth gives him only momentary trouble. We have no sense that anything is really at stake, our concern is in no way engaged, we can be in no suspense.

Why do it this way, then? For the scene is an odd one. We are used to *intermedii* and dumbshows and plays within plays; to dramatized dreams, hallucinations, visions; to magical apparitions and evocations; but our best dramatists have always led us to expect that these will make some sense in the action. We do not object when Shakespeare sets before us the Show of Kings in *Macbeth,* for this is the Witches' magic; nor to the magical show in *The Tempest,* nor the Ghost in *Hamlet;* all of these arise quite naturally out of the action. But the Tempter business is another matter. If it is something within Becket's mind, how can the women of Canterbury and the Priests witness it? They do, mind you; Becket tells them, "Watch." Are we to suppose that the Archbishop is performing magic? If not, what have we here? Eliot offers no answer to that question.

Yet the work has a certain power. How can that be? The answer is as easy as sainthood. Eliot exerts many and powerful lyric devices to do what he cannot do dramatically. He raises and allays emotions in us by his choruses, his lyric colloquies; not by his framing of the action. The piece is simply an extended lyric poem (a very fine one!) in which the object of the poet's emotion, rather than being the west wind or the skylark, is a kind of story. But it is not a dramatic advance, as Eliot and others seem to think it; if we think of it as drama, it is rather a setting back of the dramatic clock to the choric spectacles of Phrynichus. Or rather, it is less sophisticated than that must have been: it is—to speak more precisely—the medieval didactic dramatic *exemplum,* in particular the kind that set forth saints' lives; and its only real distinction from even the cruder efforts of this kind lies in the extreme beauty of the verses.

Is tragedy possible in the present time?

A very common belief is that it is not, for the reason that kings and nobles have lost their aura of dignity. This seems to me utterly trivial. It is perfectly possible to make a person in ordinary, even low station in life into a tragic figure; and it is possible to load the stage with kings and nobles and not have tragedy. It is not the natural subject which makes tragedy or comedy, it is the conceived subject matter, the dramatic conception, and the kind of art which is exerted to realize it. Shakespeare makes *Othello* out of Cinthio's melo-dramatic tale—a mere crime story—not by altering the social status of Othello and Desdemona, but by altering their characters and the moral quality of their actions; and O'Neill fails to achieve tragedy in *Mourning Becomes Electra,* not because he transports the characters of the *Oresteia* to New England and strips them of their royal raiment and rank, but because he debases them. The conception of Shakespeare is elevated; the conception of O'Neill is not.

It is also often said that tragedy and similar forms are impossible in our age because we have lost our sense of standards, or have become so cynical that we cannot believe in moral elevation, or have become so divided in our beliefs that what is tragic for some is comic for others. These notions have been echoed back and forth for some decades now; it is time that we should say something which should have been said in the first place: *Produce the evidence.* An elaborate counter-argument might easily be provided, but I believe it is unnecessary. The mere fact that the great tragedies of the past continue to have their powerful effects upon us is sufficient to disprove all such hypotheses; for were these hypotheses true, such effect would be impossible.

Indeed, I can find no real reason why we should not have tragedy in our time, except that it fell into the hands of poets who were not dramatists and thus came into disrepute, while the dramatists themselves were both repelled by what the poets were doing and attracted by the possibilities of realistic drama in prose. The dramatists can hardly be blamed; a few pages of Stephen Phillips' *Aylmer's Secret* or *Ulysses* or Richard Le Gallienne's *Orestes* are enough to make one wish that neither poetry nor tragedy had ever been invented. But mis-handling does not obviate the possibility of good handling, as abuse does not preclude use.

If there is no reason why we should not have tragedy, is there any reason why we *should* have it? It is customary to become very eloquent in arguments of this sort and to make all sorts of extravagant claims. I do not really think that civilization will collapse because a given art is not being practised, or that man will forget the great dignity of man. Candidly, I can

find only two reasons why the tragic art should be re-
vived. Tragedy offers the dramatist greater scope for
his genius; and it offers audiences a superior kind of
pleasure, one which no other art can give. These are
very simple reasons, but they seem to me quite enough.

Even so, I should want to qualify. I do not want all
dramatists to drop what they are doing and take up
tragedy; I merely want those who have a gift for tragedy to realize that there is no reason why they should
not use it. I am not suggesting that they should model
upon the great tragedies of the past, but that they
should attempt to discover what may be great tragedy
in the future. I am not suggesting that serious drama
be bound by the past, but that it should be liberated
from the immediate past. Far from calling for a new
conservatism, I propose a new revolution; an extension, not a contraction, of the dramatic arts.

Would the new tragedy be poetic drama? Does poetry
belong in the theatre? Does verse belong in it?

I think that this, too, requires a qualified answer.
Poetry and verse belong in the theatre only when the
play itself demands them, and when the dramatist is
one who can supply them. The late Maxwell Ander-
son's plays never seemed to me to demand verse, and
I cannot feel that the verse did anything whatsoever
for them. The few specimens we have of George Bernard Shaw's dramatic verse convince me absolutely
that he should always have written in prose.

And I think we have to be clear about what we mean
by poetry and verse. Poetry is not made poetry by the
fact that it involves poetic diction. The shoe is on
the other foot: poetic diction is made poetic by the

fact that it has been used to make a poem. It is generally thought that poetic diction consists of some special vocabulary of poetic words, or some special kind of style, or language involving the use of some special device such as metaphor, symbol, irony, paradox, or ambiguity. I shall not argue against these views; the history of poetry has done that for me. The history of poetry offers no evidence whatsoever that any word or style or device of language is *per se* inadmissible to poetry, or that any is *per se* constitutive of poetry. Good poetry has been written in every conceivable kind of diction; conversely, the mere use of a given diction has never been sufficient in itself to produce poetry. This is plain fact, whereas all the hypotheses about poetic diction are only hypotheses; and one fact nullifies absolutely any hypotheses to the contrary.

I should no more like to see the theatre invaded by bombast—on the pretext that it was "tragic" diction or "exalted style"—than I should like to see it invaded by another string of *Catos, Irenes,* or imitations of Shakespeare or the Greeks. Tragedy demands a high style, certainly; but the true high style is simply that which is appropriate to the tragic character—one, that is, which manifests his dignity. It is not bombast. The most affecting passages in the mature Shakespeare are composed in extremely simple language, elevated only by what they manifest to us.

Eliot seems to me to be right when he insists that if poetry is to enter the theatre, it can only be as useful to the drama. Only, this view does not go far enough; I should say it can only enter as useful to the drama *in the way in which it should be useful.* There is no doubt that the poetry in *Murder in the Cathedral* is useful; but it does more than it should; it assumes the main burden of the play.

The dominant characteristic of dramatic poetry is that it is uttered in very specifically determined circumstances, by a very specifically determined character; and its chief virtue is that it be absolutely subservient to dramatic demands. It should set before us —as vividly as possible—plot, character, and thought. The same considerations apply to verse. Verse has two chief functions in the theatre—the acoustical one, of making the words carry better (this is, I think, the real secret behind "Marlowe's mighty line"), and the dramatic function proper, of imitating as closely as possible the inflections, accents, and rhythms of speech, where these are signs of character, thought, or emotion. Verse gives the playwright much greater control over the actors than does prose. Shaw complained that whereas there was only one way of writing "Yes" or "No," there were fifty ways of saying one and five hundred ways of saying the other. A good poet does not have that difficulty. But verse should be used only when the dramatist has thought about his characters and their thoughts and emotions to the point where he must insist that their speeches be delivered in a particular way. Otherwise verse, and poetic diction too, will be useless appendages to the play, and perhaps hostile to its effect.

And, to wind the matter up: verse and diction are not essential to the theatre—in fact, we saw long ago that even language itself was not. But the greatest effects are impossible without them; and a drama which does not involve them must always fall short of those greatest effects.

Index

264

Index

Index

The manuscript was edited by Barbara Woodward and the book was designed by Sylvia Winter. Linotype Baskerville and foundry Baskerville are the typefaces. This type design is based upon type originally cut by the English printer John Baskerville about 1750. The book is printed on Warren's No. 66 Antique paper and bound in Kingston cloth from the Holliston Mills.

Manufactured in the United States of America.